Fo

MW01165803

Stories of a Season of Life
on a Family Farm

KEN PIERPONT

For more information on
Ken Pierpont's writing and ministry go to:
KenPierpont.com
Or follow Ken on Twitter:
@kenpierpont

DEDICATION

Dedicated to by siblings who enjoyed the farm with me;
Melony Evans, Pastor Kevin A. Pierpont and Pastor Nathan
Shipley Pierpont and to the Creator and Controller of the
Universe, our Blessed Lord Jesus Christ who made it.

CONTENTS

Prologue:
AUTUMN REVERIE

A red Jeep drives north along the North Fork of the Licking River in Licking County, Ohio. It is in the fall of the year—a bright October early evening. There is a snap in the air and the sky is a deep shade of blue. The Jeep turns east off State Route 13 in the village of St. Louisville and growls through the gears toward a range of hills along the eastern horizon.

It is the very peak of autumn. This time of year the road is lined with tall goldenrod, cattails and orange bittersweet. It narrows and turns from blacktop to gravel. The Jeep slows. Its driver is in no hurry. The bright Jeep winds steadily back in among the hills mottled with colorful maples, brown and rust oaks, and flaming sumac. A few miles east of the village the Jeep pauses beside the remnant of a split-rail fence overlooking a small valley and beyond where a huge pine tree grows in the banks of a crooked creek. Beyond the tree further down the valley is a small pond. Up the hill from the pond are three stately hickory trees.

After about twenty minutes the Jeep descends the valley and stops where the road follows a shelf of earth that rings the base of a high green hill. A middle-aged man unfolds himself and stretches from a long drive. He makes his way along the road with a walking stick and then down an old lane until he is standing at the base of the huge pine. He removes his hat and looks up into the green of the tree for a long time without moving. He is remembering.

Looking on you would never know that for many years the fields now grown over with multiflora rose and saplings had once been a well-maintained pasture—the surrounding acreage a working farm. At one time there had been corn-cribs, a milk house, a barn for hay, a hog barn, a garage, a silo, and in the center of it all—shaded by a majestic maple tree—a large, white, two-story farmhouse. They are all gone now. Everything but the spruce and the spring run.

Birds flit among the branches of the huge spruce. The man has not been here for many, many autumns. He closes his eyes and remembers. The sun will soon rest on the hills in the west. The air is cooling. Leaves blow across the spring run.

He looks past the tree and in his memory he is on the porch of the white farm house. His little brothers are tumbling in the leaves at the base of an old maple now gone. Soon the boys will be called in for supper but they will linger until the last streak of sun flees the sky.

In his memory, a small gray tractor comes around the corner of the barn. An old man gets off the tractor and saunters across the yard with his head cocked to the side and the collar of his blanket-lined chore coat turned up against the wind. It is his grandfather now gone almost thirty years.

Then like the light of the autumn day the pictures fade. He puts his hat back on his head, walks back to the Jeep, and drives slowly away back over the hill, the way of the setting sun.

Introduction:
TO MY HEIRS

Dear children and heirs,

This collection of stories was written with you in mind, though I pray many will read these stories over your shoulder. The stories here were written over about two decades and they don't follow a strict timeline. I wrote them down as they tumbled out of my memory after cherishing them in my heart for many years. As you know many of these stories made their way into my messages. Some of you will find yourself finishing my sentences out of your memory of my telling them on a summer evening at camp or by a fragrant fire or on a long road trip. I hope you hear my voice in them and it pleases you.

I cherish in my heart a hope that many, many generations of Pierponts will follow hard after God. The consuming desire of my life has been to follow God all the days of my life and to inspire each of you to do the same. Nothing else really matters. I don't care if you make a name for yourself. It is not my desire for you to make a lot of money or live for pleasures and comforts. More than anything else I simply want my children and the generations to follow to know God and live for Him.

There is no ultimate satisfaction in anything else. There never has been and there never will be.

I wish I could take each of you to the farm of my boyhood. Maybe on those long Monday drives through Amish Country that is what I was trying to do. But the farm as I knew it is gone. To see it today you would never know what it was like, so I have gone back into my memories so you can "see" it too.

As long as I can remember I've had a compulsion to write. When I began to write my stories my mind for some reason would travel back over the years and across the miles to the old, white, farmhouse snug in a valley off a gravel road in southeast central Ohio. Maybe one reason is because we moved a lot and the farm was a constant that changed very little in the years I was growing up. Times at the farm were happy times; holidays and vacations and reunions, so they stood out in my mind and lodge in my heart to this day.

The countryside around the farm was the kind of country that stays in your heart. Because we didn't live there all the time, or because of some mystical genetic tug, the country there was my heartland and I suppose it is to this day. To go there was to encounter nature, beautiful countryside, and gentle foothills. In the summer the place was verdant with life, in the autumn it was splashed with color, in the winter it was a daring adventure, and in the springtime it was a breath of life. Oh how often I have longed to go back to that place and back to that time.

They say that every man has his heartland. I have adopted the State of Michigan—the great Mitten State. I have fallen in love with its cool summers and its colorful autumns. I have tasted of its abundant fruit and gazed long on its sweet-water oceans. I don't even mind its long winters—they make the cherries of springtime sweeter. I have watched the sun sink into the blue water from high on Empire Bluff. From where I stood I could see South Manitou and the Empire light, the sun sinking down and the moon rising over my shoulder into the southeast sky—purple with dusk. We've biked around Mackinac Island and watched the sun set beyond the great span that connects the Michigan peninsulas. We've caught fish in its pure rivers. We've been chased by bats on an evening walk. We've watched in silent wonder the Aurora Borealis on the margin of a winter lake. We've skipped rocks and body-surfed along the unbroken miles of America's wonderful Third Coast. It's a spectacular land in places. How can you not love Michigan?

I have found the parish I intend to pour the rest of my life into—the Downriver area of Michigan south of Detroit where hundreds of thousands of people live and work. I am pastoring a fine, faithful church here on a great thoroughfare where thousands of people pass every week. I preach to hundreds of people every week. I help them see

God and walk with God. I am where I belong. But deep in my heart is Ohio, the state of my birth, and in particular, the cluster of Ohio's counties that begin to roll—Knox, Holmes, Coshocton, and Licking County.

The Farm was in Licking County northeast of Newark, the county seat, and southeast of Utica, the nearest village of any size. It was nestled in a little valley east of St. Louisville.

St. Louisville is a humble burg, a gathering of a few dozen homes where the railroad, State Route 13, and the North Fork of the Licking River all run north and south.

On the way to the farm from north and west the drive would take us across flat farm landscape. East of Columbus the land began to roll a little. In Licking County on the north side of Newark, looking east from State Route 13 the first foothills became visible. To me, those hills have an indescribable beauty and charm. The memory of them floods my heart with warmth. I have seen snow-capped mountains and stunning rocky crags. I have seen roaring rivers in rocky canyons in the Rockies in the US and Canada. I've enjoyed the Adirondacks, the Appalachians, the Blue Ridge, and the Smokies. I've even travelled along the Sierra Madre Mountain Range in Mexico, but none of these mountain ranges stir me in the same way as those simple dark humps of earth in my homeland of Ohio.

The earthly remains of Charles Pierpont and his son William Pierpont, his grandson Kenneth Pierpont who was my grandfather, and their wives all rest there now in the shadow of those hills. Their graves are within fifty yards of each other just a few miles south of the home place which was on the hill north of Chatham. This was their homeland. It must have been their heartland. They all lived there and died there. I have really only visited there. In all I have lived there only about eleven or twelve of my fifty years. So maybe my love for those hills is an acquired taste —but I don't think so. When I stand on one of those hillsides on an October evening and look out across hills backed by purple hills I have an inexplicable stirring deep in me that must be more than simple love of nature and appreciation of beauty.

I don't know if I will ever go back there for more than a visit. I sometimes wonder. I wonder if I will have a place there in the New Earth one day, when Christ is King on earth and when the earth has been refined and travel is swift and time is no factor. I have learned to love and appreciate my adopted land. This land may become your heartland and the heartland of your children, but I can't imagine feeling the same way about any other place in the world.

To get to the farm we drove into Saint Louisville from the north off Route 62 or from Newark to the south. We would turn east and drive through the village. In my early years there was an old barn there. The paint was all weathered off but the barn was half-covered with years of

Ohio license plates. In the years of my childhood the State of Ohio issued a new plate every year. The collection made a quaint and colorful welcome to the village.

In a few blocks we were on our way to the base of the first line of hills. The road turned among the hills and came to a "Y" in about a mile. I think they call the road Stickle Road now. I'm not sure they always did. We turned left and climbed a hill with a sharp curve at the top. At the base of the hill the road crossed Martinsburg Road and continued on to another fork. We took another left past a house that was usually yellow. I think a lady named Sadie lived there because my grandfather always called it Sadie's Hill. My grandpa made up his own names for things. Later I was surprised that other people did not know the names he attached to places.

The road turned again past the Berger home and then ascended the last hill before the farm. The gravel road narrowed there so much that it was our tradition to sound our horn to warn oncoming traffic. (Though I never really ever remember meeting anyone on the road there). To the right at the crest of the hill there was a beautiful old split-rail fence weathered by the years marking the margin of my grandfather's farm.

In the valley to the left just across the spring run set the square old white house. The sight of it was always so dear to us that we broke into cheering when it came into sight.

There was a time that stands out in my memory. I was in the seventh grade. We had moved to Oklahoma. We all remember it as a terrible experience. One night we just got sick of it. It was late September and hot as August back home. We were sitting around sweating and complaining one night and Dad just announced that we were going back to Ohio. In a few hours we all got in the car and just drove out of town. We were ecstatic to be going back to Ohio. We drove to Tulsa and stopped to eat. Sitting in the parking lot of a hamburger stand my folks had second thoughts about leaving without bringing things to proper closure. We kids sat in back quietly eating and listening to our parents conversation as they came to the conclusion that they needed to go back. We were sick with disappointment. They drove back to Oklahoma City that night.

Dad made the proper arrangements and in two weeks we all loaded up again and made the move. When we crossed back into Ohio we all celebrated wildly. Within a few hours we were making our way along the gravel roads to our beloved farm. It was cool October. The leaves swirled down and the air was wonderfully cold. It seemed like a holiday to us. We were so glad to be in Ohio and so happy to be staying at the farm. We enrolled in school in Utica and rode the school bus through the autumn countryside to and from school.

We lived on the farm until we got our own home a few weeks later. I rode the school bus along the winding gravel back roads to the farm gulping down the cool autumn air. There was something beautiful about seeing the bright yellow bus crawl along the hillsides among fields of ripened corn and the brilliant maples of October. To me it was like heaven in comparison to the strange land where we tried to live in a big, flat city, in a small unremarkable house among strangers. No one had taken the trouble to give the streets there decent names. They were numbered. Our bodies were there and we tried to adjust but our hearts were never in it.

The farmhouse wasn't empty or occupied by strangers. The name on the mailbox was our own name, Pierpont. The people who lived there were our people. We could be ourselves with them without being misunderstood. We could speak our heart without fear of censure. It was a safe, warm, simple, wonderful place. There was always food there and the coffee was on.

I don't want to idealize things overmuch. The coffee was truly wretched. The only way to tolerate it was to mix into it equal parts of milk and sugar. I don't think anyone ever drank it black. I'm sure it was made in the morning and cooked all day long. I was well into adulthood before I realized that coffee could taste almost as good as it smelled if you brewed good coffee fresh in the right way and you didn't let it cook or burn. But such as it was—the coffee was always on.

There were vehicles and farm implements there that took on personalities and even names and animals that made their way into our hearts and into our family lore. I didn't realize it at the time but it was there that I discovered the charm of a Ford 8N tractor. I listened to my grandfather's stories and songs. I learned about wild strawberries, mint, catnip, mushrooms, puffballs, catfish and mayapples. If I had had the sense to pay attention, I would have learned much more and this would be a longer, richer book

My grandparents and Uncle Bill and Aunt Marlene, Aunt Ann and my cousins spoke with a regional dialect that hinted of the mountains of West Virginia and Kentucky. I spent enough time in Michigan and Western Ohio that my brothers and sisters and mom did not have that sound but my dad, who was born and grew up in the county seat was the only one who sounded like that. I've been away now for years and when I do get back I am surprised and fascinated by the way the people talk.

After years away the Lord had a surprise for us. I was called to a small village church just seven miles as the crow flies from the farm I loved so much. It was in Knox County which borders Licking County on the North. There were people in the village who actually remembered my great uncle Orville and his wife Audrey. They say she had a great recipe for groundhog. She still lived a few miles away in the village of Utica.

Out on pastoral visitation one day I met a man who had grown up with my grandfather and his brothers. His name was Russell Litt and his wife's name was Paulene. They lived in a tidy white cottage right in the village of Brandon on St. Rt. 661. He had interesting stories to tell about the Pierpont boys that I had never heard before. He had vivid memories of them playing checkers on the front porch of the General Store in Chatham as young men.

A young man in our church managed a pizza place in Utica. He told me one day that there was a framed picture of my grandfather with his graduating class on the wall of the restaurant. On Monday nights the restaurant had a good special and we would often take advantage of it. Whenever we were there I would gaze on that photo of those young people. They were facing life in one of the most difficult times in American history. They would survive the Depression and they would face a great world war. At the time none of them knew it. My grandfather's young face was among them. What would he think if he had known when he posed for that picture that one day his great-grandchildren would stand and look at it on display in a pizza restaurant on the street of his home town? I wonder who will read this book who shares my blood, maybe even my last name, who I will never meet on earth?

A high-school education in those times was not to be taken for granted. In order for my grandfather to acquire one, he had to board in Utica, ride a bike, and work a special job. He did have enough time to play football. He loved to proudly proclaim that during the time that his older brother Elmer and he played football for Utica High School, no opponent ever crossed their goal line, which, oddly, he insisted on pronouncing, "gool line."

My dad and I were both named Kenneth after my grandfather. Grandpa was a farmer, a pastor, a factory-laborer, an amateur boxer, baseball player, and lay-naturalist. He was a hunter, a fisherman, an outdoorsman, and a gentleman. He was a storyteller.

He worked for over thirty years at a factory in Newark, Ohio known then as Fiberglass. Grandpa was what they now commonly call a bi-vocational pastor. He was a late-blooming pastor, ordained to the ministry by the Christian Union Church at fifty-five years old. I was very small but I remember my Grandfather's ordination service in the building they call the Tabernacle on the old conference grounds in Greenfield, Ohio.

For about the first twenty years of my life Grandpa and Grandma Pierpont owned and operated a small beef cattle farm in central Ohio. It was a modest farm. If you were to drive by on the road you would not slow down any more than the curve required. The farm occupied a hilly 110 acres. Driving past on the road you would have no way of knowing how much living and learning and laughing and loving happened on that place in the two decades it was a part of our lives. This is my attempt to tell at least a part of the story and to preserve much that was good about it.

Grandpa Pierpont was a colorful man. He was a big man for his time. He was six-foot one and weighed about two-hundred pounds. Before the influence of Christ in his life he had a quick temper and he was not reluctant to use his fists. This was greatly changed when Grandpa began to walk with the Lord, but I think it is fair to say that he never completely overcame this weakness. I always wondered if he didn't admire and subconsciously model his personality after John Wayne.

My grandpa was a changed man when he yielded his heart and will to Christ. Some things changed forever immediately. Some held stubbornly on most of his life.

He was born and raised north of Newark near the little village of Chatham. He had an older sister, Dorothy and an older brother Elmer. He also had two younger brothers named Arthur and Orville. His little sister Grace died when she was small.

He met my grandmother when they both worked at a farmer's market in Newark. Her name was Grace, too. Grace Sasser. He always called her Tiny. She was deceptively small. Until the day of her death she had eyes blue as a mountain lake. They had three children, my dad,

Kenneth Frederick, a daughter Virginia Ann, and a son named Charles William—my Uncle Bill. They raised the children in Newark, through the years of the Great Depression and the Second World War. Grandpa always longed for a farm but there would be no money for that until the children had all married and left home. That was about 1956.

Almost all the stories in this book took place on that humble farm. Woven into the stories are things I would like to pass on to my own children and grandchildren. When "choring" with grandpa on the farm he often treated us to stories of his past, our wonderful heritage. I would like to do the same.

This should be an interesting book, even for people we do not know, because within it are timeless ideas that are universally true, but for you it will be a small part of a story about a small part of your family, a part of who you are. I wish you could have been there, but since you couldn't, sit down for a while and let me tell you some stories. You will have your own places and your own people. You will have your own memories and traditions. I hope reading these memories will show you how to cherish people and places God brings along your path.

If you are reading this book and you are not a part of my family, I hope reading it tugs your heart toward home and toward God.

Chapter 1
SWEETER WHEN SHARED

There is something about love that makes sacrifice sweet. My dad understood this. He didn't talk about it he just did it. He may have learned that from his father. My grandfather worked all his life to buy his farm. He longed to raise his family on a farm but times were very hard and that would not happen. A few years after their last child married and started a family of his own he and grandma purchased a simple farm in the rolling Ohio farmland that he loved. It was a few miles from the old home place where he grew up. As far as I know they never named their farm. Upon something so wonderful, I would have bestowed a fitting name. For years we have all just referred to it as "The Farm" and that has its own charm I suppose.

Grandpa had a little Chevy. It was a small, tan, four-door Chevy Nova. Grandpa drove it for years and then it was passed around the family. It served so many of the family so faithfully that it earned a name to be proud of. It was honored with the name "Teddy" after Theodore Roosevelt who was rough and ready, a man's man. The cows were often named and some of the implements and cars earned names, but the farm was just, "The Farm."

When finally they were able to get the farm they shared it with all of us. It was our gathering place growing up for every holiday and during summer breaks. The farm was a stable thing in a life with a great deal of change. We went there to celebrate and to recover from the bitterness of defeat. We went there to be with people we loved and escape the suburbs. We went there to remember and I suppose, we went there sometimes to forget.

Thinking back I realize the farm was our vacation. It was our connection with nature, growing up mostly in places where for nature you needed to go to a park or a zoo. It was our way of appreciating and preserving our family heritage. It lent for us and I think for my dad a sense of security and stability.

I have so many memories there. If we had a big snow my cousins taught me how to sled off the huge hill across the road down onto the roadway, along the road for about a hundred yards, down the long drive that descended to the creek and across the small concrete bridge. I've never had a sled ride like it since, except for the time we almost all died trying to ride the toboggan we found on the Rutledge Road place.

In the summer we imagined the corn-crib was a pillbox that we had to capture from the enemy. We had a tire swing in an ancient maple beside the lane. We picked berries up behind the house. We worked in the haymow and we played there in the hay sometimes even though we weren't supposed to. We fished the pond and even caught fish on lines we left out all night. The first chore of the day before breakfast was "running the lines." Checking the lines would often mean fresh fish for lunch.

On summer holidays when evening came after a day of baling hay, we would all gather under the big maple and Uncle Bill would grill big fat burgers. We would eat them with baked beans and potato salad and gulp ice tea Aunt Marlene made. She was from West Virginia so her tea was sweet and that was an unusual treat for us. Then we would eat watermelon. Later we would chase fireflies. At night I remember lying on the front porch enjoying the cool misty night and looking up into the dark night sky at thousands upon thousands of stars. It was there that I had my first inklings of infinity. It was there on the porch, looking up into the galaxy that I first began to try to get my mind to understand the concept of eternity. There were no competing lights out there on the farm. It was wonderfully dark. There was a single light that stood in the yard. My grandfather called it a mercury-vapor light, but it had a switch and a kid from the suburbs could just turn it off and enjoy the darkness. I had no idea how wonderful it was to be there then. It almost hurts to think about it.

The farm economy was about to take a hard downturn but at the time there was a little profit in it so they were able to keep ahead of the payments and make a modest living.

I learned some things there too and most of them were good. It was there my grandfather taught me to drive the tractor and fish and bale hay and mow the pasture. He taught me to identify different kinds of trees and told me interesting stories of his growing up and his service in the Navy on Guam during World War II. He spent more time with the other cousins because they lived closer, but I was the first-born grandson and we shared the same name.

I didn't realize it at the time but the most valuable thing that I would ever learn from my grandfather was the art and value of storytelling. I admired him so much and you usually subconsciously imitate those you admire. He always had stories to tell. Everything reminded him of a story and he was the kind of man who just had the knack of retelling things in an interesting way and noticing things other people overlooked. Sometimes his stories surfaced in his messages. While he was preaching he would stay pretty close to his single-spaced, typewritten manuscripts, but as a child I always looked forward to the flourishes when he would launch into a story and step away from the pulpit for a while. He was especially animated and interesting and passionate then.

He told stories as he talked to friends at the grain elevator. He told stories to me as I listened from the fender of the tractor and of course he told stories at home in his recliner at night when all the adults would sit up late and I would listen until they made me go to bed. I discovered a way to listen to his stories after I went to bed, but that is a wonderful story I will tell you later.

So the farm played a major role in my life and in what I do today. We loved the farm, but it was a lifelong dream to my Grandfather.

I've never inquired about the details, but when Uncle Bill and Aunt Marlene needed a place to raise the children out in the country Grandpa let them live in the farmhouse. My cousins Diane, Beth and Lisa grew up there. Of course Uncle Bill worked the farm too to help Grandpa, though I don't think it was his real love. At the time Grandma and Grandpa moved back into town in Newark into a little duplex so the girls could grow up in the country and attend a small-town school.

Many afternoons Grandpa would get off work at Fiberglass in town and drive out to the farm to work or hunt or just tramp around the fields or putter in the outbuildings. At dark he would make his way home. On Saturday he would drive out in the morning to the farm and spend the day there. Toward evening Grandma and Grandpa would make their way back home. Grandpa would ready himself for his message and on Sunday morning he and Grandma would drive out to the little Christian Union Church in Linnville to preach.

Eventually Uncle Bill and Aunt Marlene had their own place on the farm and Grandma and Grandpa moved back into the house. I never remember anyone talking about the sacrifice that they made and I never gave it any thought until years after the farm was sold and Grandpa was with the Lord.

One day when I was back in Newark I wanted to drive past the duplex where they had lived in town when they first bought the farm. I remembered it was on Tenth Street. When I found it I was struck with the sacrifice it must have been to exchange the quiet rural tranquility of the farm for the humble neighborhood in town where the houses were built close together. Now that I am a dad and grandfather myself I understand more the way love makes sacrifice sweet.

Chapter 2
THE PLACE WHERE
I CAME TO LOVE STORIES

We almost always lived a few hours from the farm, so going there was a special event. It was an adventure and a pilgrimage. Sometimes we would arrive long after dark. After eating a bowl of cereal the adults would send us to bed. We slept in one of the big beds in one of the three bedrooms upstairs. We would try to sleep but it was hard when I knew Mom and Dad, Grandma and Grandpa, Bill and Marlene, and sometimes Aunt Ann were downstairs having a great time, telling stories, laughing and staying up later than my parents ever, ever stayed up at home.

To me it seemed wonderfully irresponsible and there was something inside me that hated the feeling of missing out. I lay in bed and listened to the voices. One night I was put to bed in the large front bedroom directly over the living room. That night I could hear the voices clearly. I sat up in bed. Toward the foot of the bed I could see a faint light shining up into the room. I got out of bed quietly to investigate.

The old house had no heating ducts running to the upstairs bedrooms. Heat radiated up the stairs and through a register cut in the floor of the bedroom. The register was at the foot of the bed. That night I noticed light and sound were rising up into the room from the register.

I got out of bed and lay on my belly and looked down into the living room. In the merciful providence of God the register was situated directly over my grandfather's chair. For some perverse reason it came to my mind to spit on his head, but I didn't want to give away my secret.

Grandpa was a storyteller. He had a way of painting pictures with words. He told of childhood memories, some of them sad and some of them silly. He told war stories of his time in the South Pacific during World War II. He told stories of his experiences as a diver, a boxer and a baseball player. He told of what it was like to live through the depression. He told of his experiences as a country pastor and he told stories from Fiberglass in Newark, Ohio where he worked for 37 years. He told stories about things that happened on the farm and colorful interesting characters he knew from the community.

They were stories I would never forget for a number of reasons. They were memorable because the man who told them was a man we all revered and loved. They were memorable because they were well-told. They were impossible to forget because so many of them were funny. Mostly, we remember them because he told them over and over again. He always seemed a little irritated if you reminded him that you had already heard a story. He would ignore you as if he was politely overlooking some embarrassing thing you did, wait a few seconds and launch back into the story.

I think most grandfathers are story tellers. The good ones, especially. Most grandpas are story tellers and most storyteller grandpas repeat the same stories over and over again. I got to thinking about that and I think I have figured out why grandpas do that. When we are young and our grandpas are old and they are telling their stories we are often waiting for them to quit because we are so busy and so important that we have to get on to all the vital issues of life like getting home to play video games, surf the Internet, or watch baseball on television. Because we are so busy and important we are often distracted and we don't listen that closely. But the Lord knows that a grandpa's stories are the very stuff of life. They are virtues and values in street clothes. They are heritage and holiness. They are faith in shirtsleeves. They are challenges and reminders custom fit for our own future and our own families.

God knew this. That is why there are so many references in Scripture to what to do when your sons and son's sons ask you questions. That is why so often in the Bible God's people were instructed to erect memorials. Here are just a few examples of the what the Bible has to say about the importance of a grandpa's stories.

Give ear, O my people, to my law;
Incline your ears to the words of my mouth.
I will open my mouth in a parable;
I will utter dark sayings of old,
Which we have heard and known,
And our fathers have told us.
*We will **not hide them from their children**,*
Telling to the generation to come the praises of the Lord,
And His strength and His wonderful
works that He has done.
For He established a testimony in Jacob,
And appointed a law in Israel,
Which He commanded our fathers,
*That they should **make them known to their children;***
That the generation to come might know them,
The children who would be born,
*That they may **arise and declare them to their children**,*
That they may set their hope in God,
And not forget the works of God,
But keep His commandments; (Psalm 78:1-7 NKJV)

One generation shall praise Your works to another,
And shall declare Your mighty acts.
(Psalm 145:4 NKJV)

Only take heed to yourself, and diligently keep yourself,
lest you forget the things your eyes have seen, and lest they
depart from your heart all the days of your life. And

teach them to your children and your grandchildren...
(Deuteronomy 4:9 NKJV)

... this may be a sign among you when your children ask in time to come, saying, 'What do these stones mean to you?' [7] Then you shall answer them that the waters of the Jordan were cut off before the ark of the covenant of the LORD; when it crossed over the Jordan, the waters of the Jordan were cut off. And **these stones shall be for a memorial** *to the children of Israel forever."*
(Joshua 4:6-7 NKJV)

Then he spoke to the children of Israel, saying: **"When your children ask their fathers** *in time to come, saying, 'What are these stones?' [22] then you shall* **let your children know,** *saying, 'Israel crossed over this Jordan on dry land'; [23] for the LORD your God dried up the waters of the Jordan before you until you had crossed over, as the LORD your God did to the Red Sea, which He dried up before us until we had crossed over, [24] that all the peoples of the earth may know the hand of the LORD, that it is mighty, that you may fear the LORD your God forever." *(Joshua 4:21-24 NKJV)

Tell your children about it,
Let your children tell their children,
And their children another generation.
(Joel 1:3 NKJV)

During his earthly life Jesus was a storyteller. Matthew 13:34 says that from that point forward Jesus never preached without telling stories. It was prophesied that Jesus would be a storyteller in Psalm 78.

So stories are more important than we realize. And to God a grandpa's stories are a very important matter. Maybe that is why grandpas repeat the same stories over and over again, because God knew that we wouldn't have the good sense to realize what a priceless heirloom those stories are until we were older and by then grandpa won't be out on the porch telling stories any more.

If my grandpas were still living I would cancel everything and go visit them with a digital recorder and I would never say, "You already told me this one, Grandpa." I would just figure this must be an important story because God has arranged for me to hear it over and over again. And I would listen close so I could repeat it to my grandchildren some day... over and over again.

Now also when I am old and grayheaded,
O God, do not forsake me,
*Until I **declare Your strength to this generation**,*
Your power to everyone who is to come.
(Psalm 71:18 NKJV)

That is why I have written this book. These stories are the most valuable thing I have to give you after the great, life-changing story of the gospel. Somehow I think these stories are stories that help the story of the gospel make sense to us.

Sometimes in the summer we all attended a church conference in southern Ohio together. All the men would sleep in a simple old building built long and low like a barracks. They called the meeting Christian Union Council. At day's end, lying in their cots before sleep, one of the old preachers would play his harmonica.

His name was Sooter Hoople, it really was, and he was a bachelor pastor. He had a brother named Harry. They were from southern Ohio where the hills roll from Interstate 70 south to the Ohio River. Every year he volunteered to be a counselor at the Christian Union Camp in Greenfield, Ohio. He did this for years and years. He was a counselor when I was a camper. When I became a counselor, he was still a counselor. Long after I had moved on to marriage and ministry he was a counselor year after year.

We would return to the Christian Union Campgrounds for a week in August for the annual assembly they called Christian Union Council, too. Grown-ups would invade the camp for a week for a combination of old-fashioned camp meeting and denominational convention. Christian Union Council was a humble affair but I loved it. We enjoyed common meals, singing, spirited preaching, and fellowship with other Christians. There were other kids to play with. In the evening after the Vesper Service in the Tabernacle, they would open the Canteen and we would get a soft-drink and a snack and stand around in the cool evening and visit. Sooter Hoople and his brother Harry were always among the pastors and laymen that attended Council.

Sooter Hoople was a happy character who loved children. He always wore a smile. He was a small man. His hair was white the whole time I knew him. Late in the evening after lights-out when things got quiet, Sooter Hoople would stroll down the aisle between the rows of beds and play the harmonica to put the boys to sleep. He played an old Echo Harp, the big one. The sound carried up and down the rows of cots in the boys' dorm and then tapered into the sound of crickets and summer nighttime.

We would lay in our bunks spent from the day. Cool would creep through the uninsulated walls. Fireflies would hover over the grass outside. The moon would rise and the dew would settle. One by one our breathing slowed with sleep.

Sometimes when I think about Sooter Hoople and his simple harmonica I pity children today whose lives are so noisy with electronic gadgets, media, music and movies. I wonder if they ever stop and listen to crickets in the night or lay on the bank on a summer afternoon and listen to a stream running over rocks. I wonder if they have ever heard anyone play old hymns on a harmonica at bedtime.

But at day's end on the Christian Union Campground after the last strain of the harmonica music faded to the sound of crickets the men would tell stories. I lay in bed listening, never saying anything, feeling secure and happy and enjoying the company of these simple Christian people. Grandpa's stories were always favorites. I could tell that Grandpa was a man people loved and admired like I did.

Maybe it was looking down through the heater grate in the old farmhouse that I first began to feel the power of stories. Maybe it was lying in my cot on the old conference grounds in Greenfield, Ohio. Maybe it was sitting in the pew in the tiny church in Linnville when I would be aroused from my daydream in the middle of the sermon when Grandpa would step off to the side of the pulpit and tell a personal story. Maybe it was in the after-school Bible clubs that my mother taught or listening to Aunt Bea on Children's Bible Hour, or listening to Dad's preaching. (Isn't it always the stories that we remember most about preaching?). It was probably all the above, but I came to love stories and storytelling. I always cringe when I hear well-meaning preachers say that preachers should not be story tellers. Will there ever be a more powerful preacher on earth than Jesus? Was Jesus not a story teller?

I believe in the power of stories. I love to listen to them. I love to read them. I love to collect them. I love to write them. I love to tell them. I believe the eternal destiny of a person's soul turns on the power of a story. That story is called the Gospel. It is the story of Jesus, why He lived, where He came from, and why He died and rose again. I believe in the power of stories to change people for the better. I believe in the power of stories to inspire acts of service and sacrifice. I believe in the power of stories to stir men and women to loyalty and love.

My brother, Nathan has written a song about it. He calls it "The Story of Christ," and in the song he sings, "It's the story that's changed all our lives," and it has.

There is something in me that longs to express itself in stories. Brew some coffee, friend, put another log on the fire, pull up a chair, and keep reading. I have more stories to tell.

Chapter 3
OF TREES AND TRUTHFULNESS

Though I had been in the ministry since I was seventeen, I was almost thirty years old when I was called to serve my first full-time solo pastorate. It was a small village church only a few miles from the farm. I wanted the family to see it. The farm was no longer in the family and I had not been there for many, many years.

We made the farm a day-off destination. Off the main highway we wended through the countryside on familiar gravel roads. Every mile was a treasury of memories and stories to tell. We climbed Sadie's Hill which was always such an adventure in the winter, passed the Berger's place and then rounded the last bend before the farm would come into view.

So much had changed. The pond seemed so much smaller than I remembered. The raspberry patch behind the house was gone. My favorite tire swing was missing from the big maple across the lane from the house. Some of the outbuildings had given way to the years. The farm was not as I remembered it, but one thing caused me to catch my breath in surprise.

At Christmas time we would always crowd toward the window of the car as we took the last turn in the road. The farm lay in the valley below and we would strain to see the lights on the little evergreen beside the spring run. One Thanksgiving I remember helping Grandpa decorate the tree with a six-foot stepladder.

The tree was still there, but it towered over the old two-story farmhouse. The little spruce by the spring run was now over forty feet high!

The next time the family was together, I told Grandma about how the tree had grown. Dad laughed and assuming a Paul Harvey-like voice said; "How would you like me to tell you the rest of the story?"

Years ago Dad and his younger brother Bill skipped school on the opening day of rabbit season to hunt with Grandpa. Grandpa gave his approval on the condition that the boys would not lie when asked the reason for their absence. They took the deal and skipped school to hunt rabbits with their dad. Evening came quickly and after a nice dinner with fresh meat the boys tumbled into bed, but they would face the judgment at school the next day.

They weren't alone. The boys were called upon to account for their absence the following day. They joined a long line of boys at the principal's office. Most of the other boys claimed they were sick. (They were sick of having to go to school on opening day of rabbit season.) Dad and Bill, true to their word, told the truth.

"We were rabbit hunting with our dad," they said.

"Are you sure you weren't feeling just a little under the weather, boys?" the principal asked.

"No sir, we were feeling fine, and we were rabbit hunting with our dad."

The gavel dropped and the sentence came swiftly. They would stay after school one hour each night until they had made up the time they had missed.

On the final day of Dad's punishment the teacher, out of sympathy, walked back the aisle where dad was sitting and gave him a little gift. It was a tiny start of an evergreen tree in a cut-off milk carton. It didn't seem like much of a compensation for the suffering he endured, but he carried it home. That night Grandpa and Dad set it out in the backyard of their home on Bowers Avenue in Newark, Ohio.

A few years later Dad was serving in the Navy in Korea, Bill and Aunt Ann were married and gone. My grandfather realized a lifelong dream. He and Grandma found the little farm nestled in the hills north of town near where he had grown up. They moved to the farm and when they did Grandpa took the time to carefully transplant the little pine from the yard in Newark to the bank of the spring run on the farm in front of the house.

It's always been a source of beauty. It's a haven for birds. In the winter its branches are flocked with snow and and at Christmas they glow with multi-colored lights. It's fed year round by the spring at its feet. But I know that it is more than that. It is a forty foot tall monument to the virtue of truthfulness.

Maybe someday I will go back and follow the gravel roads to the old farm. I'll introduce myself to the current owners and tell them about the priceless monument they have growing in their front yard. I hope by telling the story here I will inspire my children and grandchildren with the timeless value of virtues that only Christ by the progressive work of the Spirit within can produce, like faith, honor, honesty and truthfulness.

> *"The truthful lip shall be established forever, but a lying tongue is but for a moment." (Proverbs 12:19 NKJV)*

Chapter 4
THINKING AND FEELING

Childhood and youth can be a confusing time. Trying to get the knot of youth untangled is hard if you are alone. It's best if there are loving people around helping you when you are trying to do that. If you have some simple, safe, and beautiful places to do that you are blessed indeed. The farm was a place like that for me when I was trying to untangle the knots of youth.

Sometimes I don't think. I always *feel* but sometimes I just don't think. I drive right past where I'm going sometimes without thinking because I'm talking to someone or to myself, or listening to the radio, or chatting on the cell phone, or listening to my iPod, or noticing people, or looking at trees and flowers, or listening to birds. I sort of "feel" my way through life and forget to think.

I've been this way for as long as I can remember. One summer I worked for a couple weeks on the farm with Grandpa. He was mostly a thinker... a real good thinker. That summer I think he took on the project of helping me learn to think some.

In the morning we would "run the lines" down at the pond to see if we got any fish during the night, then we would do the chores. After the chores we would sit down to breakfast. Grandpa would go over the day's work and expect me to remember the details and the sequence of the work. Usually I would forget...just too many wonderful distractions everywhere I looked—too many things to feel to do much thinking.

One day over lunch Grandpa went over the afternoon work. I paid little attention. I was distracted by fried catfish, fried mushrooms, and fried puffballs. I was distracted by piles of buttery-fresh calico sweet corn crisp from the garden. I was distracted by garden ripe fresh tomatoes. I gave lunch my full attention. It just felt right at the time. Between Grandpa and me we turned a huge platter of sweet corn into a pile of furry cobs, cleaned up, and headed for the afternoon work.

We walked together across the yard. Grandpa got up in the tractor seat. I jumped on the wagon. He started the tractor—I whistled for the dogs. I leaned my head back and smelled the good farm air. My stomach was full, my heart was light and all was right with the world. I forgot what Grandpa said we were supposed to be doing—but that didn't matter. I was a fifteen year old boy on the farm with an afternoon of work and an evening of fishing ahead of me.

At night I would lay on the porch in awe of the night sky. When I was too tired to stay awake I would drift into secure sleep on the huge bed in the upstairs bedroom with the window open to the cool night and smell the new-mown hay or other honest farm smells on the summer night air.

Grandpa throttled up the old Ford 8N, let out the clutch, and drove away. The wagon didn't move. He was going up to bring down a load of hay so he had pulled the pin on the draw-bar on the way in to eat lunch. When he drove away the wagon tongue just fell to the ground. I stood on the wagon watching the tractor pull away. I jumped down and ran to catch up. I grabbed both fenders and jumped up onto the tow-bar.

Grandpa chuckled— "You need to pay attention and plan ahead a little, Kenny," he said.

I've been working on that now for about thirty years, but I am still a better feeler than a thinker. More and more as you age and gather experience in life you realize that God custom-made each of us. He designed us for what He destined us for and that will work out for our good and His glory.

He made me to feel things deeply. I would rather be that way than like some people I know. They think a lot but don't seem to feel much of anything. If they feel anything you really can't tell by looking at them. I suppose it's best to do some of both. Feelers ought to work on thinking and thinkers should think about feelings sometimes. Come to think of it thinking and feeling are both a big part of living. At least that's how I feel about it.

Chapter 5
STATUTE OF LIMITATIONS ON YOUTHFUL FOLLY

"Which way to the threads on a bolt run?"

"Which way do you turn a wrench to loosen a nut?"

"Who were the Axis Powers during WWII?"

"Who were the Allies?"

"What was D-Day?"

Grandpa might have had some "teacher" in him. He had the skill every good teacher has of asking questions to see if you understand what he is trying to teach you.

"What is a harvest moon?"

"What do I need to do before I take this ring off?"

"What is going to happen when you let go of that line?"

"How many different kinds of meat did I tell you were in a turtle?"

"What side of a tree does the moss grow on?"

"How can you find the North Star?"

"Does a catfish have scales?"

He should have asked; "What happens if you let the clutch out while the tractor is still in gear?" or "What happens if you let the clutch out too quickly when you have an implement attached to the tractor?" or "What happens if you fail to secure both brakes and leave the tractor idling at the top of the hill?" These would have been good questions.

In our short time together he taught me how to stack hay so it wouldn't fall off the wagon. He taught me how to pick green beans without missing any. He taught me how to catch and clean fish, including catfish. He taught me how to identify plants and stars and trees and animals and animal tracks. He taught me how to thread a bolt. He taught me how to ride a horse... well he tried to teach me how to ride a horse. He set the bar high. He expected a lot. He had a way of making you want to please him. One of the most delightful things he taught me was how to drive a tractor. I loved driving the tractor. I was a bit of a slow learner but I loved it.

One day I was not catching on too quickly and Grandpa got a little impatient and said, "Here, let me show you. Just get off."

I did what I was told, not thinking that what he really intended to say was, "Take the tractor out of gear and then get off."

I got off. When I did, I took my foot off the clutch without taking the tractor out of gear. It lurched suddenly and violently forward and died. The swift forward motion of the tire slammed into my grandpa's side and sent him sprawling to the ground.

He either had an episode of Post Traumatic Stress Disorder or faked it really well to frighten some sense into me. He fell to the ground and rolled around disoriented for a while. He was not injured, but I felt the rebuke of it and vowed inwardly never to disappoint him again.

On another occasion Grandpa let me attach the cyclebar mower and mow the pasture. He and Dad were down in the yard when, in my inexperience, I popped the clutch. I was aware they were watching me and I wanted to impress them with how swiftly I could navigate the turns and operate the mower.

The tractor lurched against the mowing implement. Dad whistled and Grandpa shouted. They were afraid I would damage the mower or flip the tractor. I knew what I had done and didn't need a rebuke, but I think it frightened both of them. Again, there was no damage or danger and I lived to tell about it. Again, I vowed not to disappoint the men I so wanted to please.

Late on a summer evening we were coming down from baling the hill on the back of the property. I was following Grandpa down the two-track lane. He was hauling the baler and a wagon-load of hay. I was following with the spare tractor. It was my responsibility to close and latch the gate at the top of the hill.

I drove the tractor through the open gate, parked it parallel with the steep hill, left the tractor running (it had no starter). I set the brakes. (I was sure I set the brakes.) I turned my back on the tractor, walked over to the gate, shut and latched it. When I turned back toward the tractor it was gone... gone.

The tractor was bounding down the hill kicking up dust in a wide arch. One brake had let go and the other held and the tractor as was bouncing wildly down the steep hill gaining speed like a carnival ride. For a moment I thought it would catch up with Grandpa—perhaps even collide with his rig, but it didn't. The tractor swept down the hill in a big circle and lost some speed when it started back up the grade. Finally it came to rest with its tires in the rut of the lane.

Come to think of it there may have been guardian angels involved.

I ran down the hill after it full speed, praying that my grandfather didn't see what had happened. I jumped onto the tractor seat, released the brake that had held, and pulled in behind Grandpa as if nothing had happened. I never told him. He never asked me. I didn't tell Dad until years later when the Statute of Limitations on such things had expired.

God protected me from any serious injury in all the dangerous things you have to do to grow to manhood, like learning to drive a car or tractor, operating equipment, navigating the choppy water of the public school system, surviving thugs and bullies, dating, courtship, and Baptist church business meetings.

By God's merciful providence and the counsel and prayers of four godly grandparents and two loving parents I survived to have children of my own. I wonder what dangers they have navigated that I will know nothing about for years?

Chapter 6
THE IGNORANCE OF
IGNORING WARNINGS

I have almost never gotten myself into trouble without over-riding at least one warning first. Sometimes I have managed to ignore a series of warnings before I plunged head-long into mischief. I have noticed there are evil influences everywhere I go and evil impulses inside me, but God is always faithful to warn me before I yield to them. Sometimes a warning comes in the still, small voice of conscience. Sometimes I hear my mother's voice in my mind. Sometimes my wife lets me know when I'm about to step in something messy. There are times when I am reading the Bible that I feel like God is speaking to me in clear, unmistakable language warning me of folly. In His infinite creativity, through a network of angels, prophets, preachers, parents, the inner voice of the Spirit, the dictates of His word, the Bible, Sunday School and church memories, or the agency of human authorities, He is faithful to warn His children when they are about to do something harmful or foolish.

The Angel of the Lord once visited a man named Balaam to warn him. This should have been a very impressive and intimidating warning but Balaam was spiritually out-to-lunch and did not see the angel in his path. This was the Angel of the Lord. We are not talking here about the naked, effeminate, chubby, cherub of the Lord, we are talking about the "I-command-all-the-armies-of-heaven", Angel of the Lord—armed with a sword.

Other places where the Angel of the Lord manifested himself, strong men were reduced to cowering fear. Balaam's donkey saw what Balaam didn't see and had the good sense not to go on. When the donkey balked, Balaam began beating him with a stick until God enabled the donkey to speak and warn him that he was in the presence of the Angel of the Lord. Can you imagine his shock?

If my donkey talked to me I think I would have been speechless, but Balaam talked back to his donkey. They had a little bickering exchange there in the presence of the Angel of the Lord.

The donkey said, "Why are you beating on me?"

Balaam said, "If I had a sword I would kill you."

The donkey said, "Haven't I been a good donkey for you all these years?"

Finally, out of pity for the poor animal, God opened Balaam's eyes. So God is faithful to warn even ignorant and unworthy people in the most creative ways. This should be a comfort to all of us.

It's unusual for God to send angels and donkeys to warn us, but it is common for Him to use grandmas and grandpas. I remember once, years ago, when God warned me very directly through my grandpa. My grandpa warned me never to play in the barn.

"The barn is not a place to play. It can be dangerous there." Of course I should have listened to him but I was influenced by my evil cousin. At least that's the way I remember it. I've really never been that good at thinking up evil things to do on my own. But it seems like there is always someone around who is good at bad stuff. My evil cousin was like that.

That old barn was one of the most fascinating places I have ever explored. There are so many interesting possibilities there. There was a rope hanging from a rafter and the barn was filled with hay so it was the most tempting thing in the world to climb onto a stack of bales and swing from the rope and drop into the hay below. I did it over and over again and so did my cousin. In fact, I'm sure it was his idea.

After a while even something as fun as that gets a little routine, so we started to look for variations. That is when Jimmy came up with a delicious idea. He casually suggested that we could swing over and land on the roof of the milk room. Immediately I knew it was something I had to do. He told me he didn't think I could do it. I said I could. He was sure I couldn't. So, of course I showed him. I climbed to the top-most bale of hay, took the rope and adding a Tarzan-like cry for effect swung out over the top of the milk room. Well out over the milk room I let go of the rope and dropped nicely onto the roof. Nothing to it, except it wasn't actually a roof, it was a ceiling.

The milk room was framed under the shed-roof of the barn and finished with drywall. When I dropped onto the roof I happened to miss the studs. I landed with all my weight directly on a piece of drywall between the studs. I shot through the drywall like a hot knife through butter—but I didn't fall to the ground. That would have been merciful compared to what happened. I missed the studs but I landed astraddle of the milking stanchion with one leg on one side and one leg on the other. The pipe brought my swift descent to a sudden, jarring, painful halt. It was a very uncomfortable position. It still hurts a little when I think about it. When the dust settled I could hear my evil cousin's hideous and sadistic laughter.

I've really never been that quick to pick up on things, but this experience left an indelible impression on my psyche. When I think back on that warm memory of my dangling from a hole in the ceiling of the milk room I'm reminded again to take warnings seriously and I'm reminded that it is a really bad idea to let myself be influenced by evil people... like my cousin Jimmy.

I always expected Jimmy to organize prison riots when he grew up or take up with the Mafia, or run for congress, but I have to admit he turned out pretty good after all. As evil as he was he probably could never overcome my influence on him for good. Hey, we all have our role to play, right?

You don't want to take my humor too seriously. My cousin was really not evil and the only part of this story that is not true and accurate is my evaluation of him as "pretty good after all." The fact is he is a fine husband, father, and provider and a leader in his church. I say this because it is true and because I don't want my aunt to scratch me off the Christmas card list or write me out of her will.

Chapter 7
ORVILLE PIERPONT

My Grandfather Pierpont grew up near Chatham, Ohio in the days when cars were a novelty of the rich. For staples and supplies that the family couldn't grow on the farm they would take a buggy to the village store. He often told the story about what happened on one of those trips to town. It was winter. The river was frozen and the ground was covered with snow. The trip to Chatham would be an adventure that winter day. They would use the sleigh. The whole family clamored to go.

After all the necessary items were bought, sometimes there was money for something special. What the boys longed for most was a treat originally called Elijah's Manna in 1904. Clergymen objected (those obstreperous clergymen). C. W. Post countered, defending his use of the name, but the controversy didn't die until the cereal was banned in England and eventually re-issued under its new name: Post Toasties. The company discontinued the cereal in 2006. Why would anyone eat Post Toasties anyway when they could begin their day with a glorious bowl of Cinnamon Toast Crunch? But in the years of my grandfather's boyhood, cars were rare and Cinnamon

Toast Crunch would not come along until years after his death.

My grandfather was born in 1908. Ohio's first radio station was in 1922. If that signal reached Chatham, the Pierpont boys could not have listened. He had moved into town before rural electrification reached northern Licking County. Grandpa would live through two world wars, serving in one, the Korean and Vietnam conflicts, and the Great Depression. A little over a decade before his death one summer night in June, Americans had strolled on the surface of the moon. My grandfather lived through polyester double-knit suits, platform shoes, disco music and the moon race, but the invention that captured the interest of the oldest Pierpont boys during those days was made in Battle Creek, Michigan and sold in boxes at the store in Chatham—corn flakes called Post Toasties.

The store and the Methodist Church in Chatham would be significant in the social life of the Pierpont brothers. They tell me the Pierpont boys gathered on the porch of the store to swap stories and play checkers. I never remember my grandfather losing a game of checkers.

The place the family lived at the time still known by the name of the previous owners: The Green Place set back from the North Fork of the Licking River about a half mile. Not far from there the the river crossed the road—or the road passed through the river. On this day the river had a sheet of ice. The trip to town went well. The family attended church and then stopped at the store to get the things they would need for the week and made their way south toward home until they go to the place where the road ran through the river.

Halfway across the river the horse lurched and my great grandmother Lilley was thrown from the sleigh. She was holding my grandfather's youngest brother, baby Orville. She lost her grip on the baby and he was plunged into the ice water.

My grandpa was about ten at the time. His brother Elmer was twelve. They were able to make their way to safety on the bank. The parents stayed in the ice-clotted river trying desperately to save baby Orville. He was in the water along with all the contents of the sleigh.

What happened next would live in Grandpa's memory for the rest of his life. Orville was rescued alive from the water. He recovered from the incident and went on to live to old age and died in 1989.

As a young man Orville slipped and fell, injuring himself. The injury probably contributed to his noticeably hunched back. His handicap did not keep him from being active and productive. Around nearby Utica, Ohio for years if you needed a man to fix a car no one else could fix, you took it to Orville Pierpont. He could usually dope it out. He had a neat place at the crest of a hill west of town. Behind the house he had built a small trout pond.

When I visited as a boy he would take me out back and throw rabbit food in and trout would churn the water. Nonetheless Orville lived to marry, raise a family, and earn an honest living doing something helpful. All that and a wife who knew how to fix groundhog. Despite the trauma, he lived a good life.

The part of the story my grandpa loved to tell was what happened there on the bank of the river while Orville was bobbing in the icy water. His brother Elmer's concern was that the new groceries were thrown into the water and they were being carried downstream. Elmer, seeing the gravity of the situation began to call out instructions from the bank. Grandpa remembered his exact words sixty years later. He was shouting at the top of his lungs to anyone who would listen; "Hey, Save the Post Toasties. Somebody, save the Post Toasties." I asked Grandpa if anyone did. He said he didn't remember that.

Orville's icy plunge happened over eighty years ago. Elmer died before I was born and this little incident is about all I know of him. I'm sure he lived to regret his misplaced priorities. Buggies and sleighs have been replaced by automobiles and hundreds of other brands of cereal have captured the enthusiasm of children now, but scrambled values are still a common problem. It would be funny if it weren't so tragic.

Since Elmer was only twelve at the time we can forgive him for being more concerned about his Post Toasties than his baby brother, but once we're old enough to know better, we should no longer value things over people, profit over principle, and time over eternity. We shouldn't waste our time worrying about things that don't matter or working overtime for things we will sell for small change at a garage sale or haul off to the second-hand store in a year or two.

I hope none of you ever forget what a treasure people are—especially your family. They are better than Post-Toasties and Cinnamon Toast Crunch.

Chapter 8
ONE MORE CAST

I've never been that patient or particularly skilled at
fishing. Good fishermen need at least a little of both.
When I was a boy I liked to spend the evening on the
margin of the pond with my Zebco 404 rod and reel
combination. I would cast and retrieve over and over again
as fast as I could. My Dad, my Uncle Bill, and Grandpa
always said I needed to sit still and watch my bobber for a
while but I was able pass my entire childhood from birth
to about my sophomore year of Senior High School
without ever sitting still. I'm writing this standing up.

One mellow late June evening I was standing on the
south edge of the pond casting a purple night crawler into
the water and reeling it in over and over again. The sun was
dropping over the hill in the west and glowing in the tops
of the huge hickory trees up the hill to the north.

I hadn't had a nibble all evening. I could see there were
people on the porch of the house and I wondered what
they were doing. My sister or my brothers or my cousins
had something going, so I decided that I would make one
more cast and then reel in my line and hike back to see
what was going on.

I cast out the purple worm for the last time and watched it for a second, then losing patience I began to retrieve my bait as fast as I could. I cranked on the reel yanking the tip of the pole up and down with each rotation, pulling the bobber and worm fast toward shore. Just when the bobber reached the point where I would jerk it from the water, a terrific splash churned the water just behind it and the line went tight. My prize was a nice fat bass. Everyone was impressed. No one guessed I landed it without patience or skill.

Every once in awhile on a perfect summer night when a boy is flailing the water all the wrong way, with all the wrong bait, providence will smile on him in spite of himself. He will hook into a fish that will still live in his memory when his sons have sons.

Things haven't changed much since that summer night long ago. My equipment is a little more costly and sophisticated but I'm still as impatient as ever when I fish and I don't care as much about catching things as I do about being out in God's world while the sun slips from sight and the moon rises.

Like most men I like to have something to do with my hands to justify an evening outdoors. I still like going out and listening to water run over rocks. I still like being outdoors on a summer evening watching trout rise and listening to crickets. I'm a social guy and my life is people, but from time to time in order to have anything worth giving to the people I love and serve, I find that I need some time in a quiet place where the phone will not ring.

And there are always lessons to learn outdoors. I learned something important that summer evening on the bank of my grandpa's pond. You may not be that good or that patient, but sometimes the catch of a lifetime will come your way if you just try one more time before you reel in your bait.

Chapter 9
TRUTH SEED AND HEART SOIL

I don't know where your life has taken you or in what part of this great earth God has placed you. Even if the Lord leads you to serve in a place that is teeming with people He treasures, I hope you still live within access of some countryside. If you do, get in your car some evening this week. Get out of town. Let the radio rest in silence for right now. Listen to the sounds of the countryside. Turn off the air conditioner and roll down all the windows. Drive slowly down a country road with the cool of evening coming on. Breathe deep and look close. Notice the honest smells of soil and living things on the evening air. Do you see it? Do you feel it? There is abundance all around you.

Field on field rises and falls before you laden with growing things. The world around you is bursting with life. Roadside stands spill over with fresh garden produce. Big, red, juicy, vine-ripened tomatoes, like you can't buy in the store. Sweet, sweet corn will only be here for a swift season. Blueberries are plump and abundant. Green beans with the life still in them, unlike the lifeless things you eat from a can the rest of the year. Leaves are large and dark shades of green. Branches of fruit trees are beginning to bend under the weight of their bounty.

That is the way I remember my grandpa's farm, except for a spot on the very top of the hill beyond the west pasture. The field there was always planted with corn or sown with hay but there was an area about the size of a small house, where nothing ever grew. It was as barren as a concrete slab, an ugly patch of dry hard earth. It was planted every year, watered, spread with fertilizer and manure and soaked with rain the same as all the other ground around it, but nothing ever grew there. It was fallow ground. It was poisoned.

Grandpa always said it was because there had been an old gas well there and when they took it out the ground was ruined by salt water. I'm not sure of all the reasons, but it was as lifeless as stone. It was especially obvious this time of the year where everything around it was in the full flush of life.

My grandpa planted crops in the ground. I plant truth in the heart. I am a communicator of truth, like my grandfather was a planter of seed. Not just any truth, God's truth, life-giving truth, truth that results in life if received and death if ignored. Truth is like the seed of life. Communicating the truth of God is a little like being a farmer. When I write or speak or counsel I am sowing seed. Like the pictures you have seen of the farmer with a sack over his shoulder broadcasting seed in a wide arch, I am broadcasting seed every day. And the seed is very good. Not because it is mine. I didn't create the seed of God's truth and I can't improve it. I can't make it grow. I just take handfuls of it every day and cast it out on the soil of people's hearts.

Some of that seed eventually becomes rich, rich produce in the garden of God. Every day I see growing things all around me, things bursting with spiritual vitality. There is evidence of spiritual growth. I hate to admit it but there are some patches of dry barren earth close at hand, too. The woman who gets preoccupied with other things and never really finds time for things that matter most. The man whose heart is hardened by pride or jealousy or closed with hurt. He doesn't realize how barren a life can be when a heart is hardened to the seed of truth. He can't hear or he won't and the life-giving seed lies dormant on the surface of his hard heart. Sometimes a person will occupy a pew for years and get soaked with the water of life, his heart will be sown with truth year after year and he will still go away hard and barren week after week.

I was not the first to notice this. Jesus told a story about it. We usually call it the four kinds of soil. In the story Satan snatches away seed, some falls on ground that is hard, some is choked to death by weeds after a fine start.

The Enemy does not want people to hear this message so he loves the hard soil of discontent or distraction. He loves to swoop down and snatch up the seed. He loves to disrupt the truth from taking root and bearing fruit in a life or a family.

Pray this never happens to you. Never stop listening to God. Never stop gathering with God's people to hear the truth of God. Never close your heart or harden your heart to the truth of God. If you do, your life will become barren and empty where there could be lush bountiful life.

Make a habit of regular public worship. Have a van load of kids and fill a pew with them every Sunday. Sing with your heart and listen with your soul and obey with all your might. Don't ever let your heart become hard and barren.

I wish I could take you back to those winding roads to the farm in Licking County on a late-summer evening. You could see and smell and hear growing things all around you. But it's hard to go back. Take a drive on a summer evening and think about what I have written here. Think about bounty and abundance and growing good things in the soil of your heart. Listen for God's voice. It's like truth seed on heart soil. Don't ever let your heart get so hard nothing grows there.

Chapter 10
BUILDING MATERIAL

Grandpa and Grandma lived through the Great Depression. Like everyone else who endured that Great American Hardship it marked them for life. They were careful and frugal and enterprising.

Grandpa loved to show us how to make homemade toys and improvise to save money. He loved to fabricate things. It was a long way to town, so he and Grandma weren't in the habit of running to town for every little thing.

When they bought gifts they were always practical. Mittens, hats, underwear were common. Their food and clothing were modest. They lived in a kind of simple luxury. They liked to spend their time and energy doing things that helped provide the necessities of life: gardening, fishing, hunting and farming.

We fished the pond and we ate the fish. Bass, crappie, catfish and bluegills. We even caught and cleaned and ate a turtle one summer. Once I caught an eleven-inch crappie. Grandpa said it was a record catch and nailed the head over the corn crib door. I guess that's just what you do. The fishing was fun, but the fishing was food.

They never owned two cars, but shared one modest standard-issue blue-collar Chevrolet with crank windows, an AM radio, and a minimum of chrome. It was only in the last decade of their lives that they allowed themselves the option of air-conditioning.

There were three huge trees that stood as sentinels on the hillside north of the pond. They were hickory trees. I knew this for two reasons. First because of the nuts that littered the ground all around the base of the trees and second because my grandfather told me so and he always taught me how to identify the trees and plants that grew around the farm.

One day my grandfather said, "You should gather those nuts up and put them in bags and sell them for Christmas. I took a box and gathered up all the nuts I could find. When I got home I put them in bags and peddled them door to door to raise money for Christmas presents.

I sold them all. Grandpa was proud of me and glad that the hickory nuts went to good use.

Just a few weeks of my life were spent with my grandfather on the farm though we visited as often as we could. Grandpa Pierpont took it upon himself to teach me things almost continuously while I was there. He taught me to catch catfish, bluegill, crappie, and bass. He taught me to catch and clean a turtle. (Did you know there are fourteen different kinds of meat in a turtle?) He showed me how to find edible puff-balls and mushrooms and fry them in batter with the fish. He tried valiantly to teach me to weed the garden and pick the green beans without missing a single one—this without any real success. He showed me how to plant trees. He inspired me to start a business selling hickory nuts.

He patiently taught me, at great peril to himself, how to dive the Massey-Ferguson, even though I was the slowest of learners. Two or three times I narrowly escaped serious disaster. He taught me to ride a pony and get back on after I was thrown to the ground. He gave me detailed lessons in meteorology most of which was over my head.

I watched in wide-eyed wordless wonder at the beginning of the calf-producing process and then, wide-eyed, I watched again as my grandfather demonstrated a few very graphic birthing techniques in the middle of one cold spring night. On the way back to my warm bed he launched into an impromptu lecture on the whole process of cattle reproduction that was memorable to say the least.

He sang old folk songs and told funny stories that it would be impossible for me to forget simply because he repeated them so often. I learned how to get a bale of hay on the wagon, even if it weighed almost as much as I did. I learned names of birds, plants, and trees. I'm sure I am the only one of my peers who knew the details of the blight that swept through the Midwest shortly after the turn of the century and in thirty-five to forty years made the American chestnut almost extinct.

Grandpa told me stories of natural history, and tales of World War II in the South Pacific—in riveting, first-person narrative. He told me stories of the antics of his youth he would have thrashed me for trying myself. He threatened me frequently with beatings and whippings, but I could not have imagined disobeying him or challenging his authority for a minute. In all his life he never laid a disciplinary hand on me. My admiration for him was boundless. The influence of those weeks on the farm was all out of proportion to the amount of time spent there.

When Grandpa needed to repair something he rarely went to the hardware or farm supply store. He salvaged and improvised and fabricated with materials he had. His workshop was piled with things he had rescued from old buildings and implements over the years. The floor of the garage was jammed with five-gallon buckets filled with parts and hardware, and fasteners and inexplicable paraphernalia that made sense only to him. I'm sure he had a good idea just where everything was. I'm sure no one else did.

He pulled boards and nails from a dilapidated shed to repair the working barn one afternoon. He taught me how to straighten nails. He showed me how to use a block to get better leverage to pull a nail from long-seasoned hardwood. He taught me a technique to keep from hammering my thumb when driving a nail or breaking my arm when driving a stake. Now I never drive a nail without thinking of him.

Grandpa started his family at the very beginning of the Great Depression. Because of that he and Grandma celebrated the day of his hiring at Owens-Corning Fiberglass until they day they died. Grandma sent him off to work there with a full lunch pail every day for thirty-five years and considered it a provision of God.

They didn't buy what they could grow. They proudly grew tomatoes, peppers (that Grandpa called mangoes), green beans, limas, corn, and cucumbers (that they always called pickles). They raised their own beef and sometimes milked their own cow. They majored in home economics long before there were formal courses on it. They shared one car and it was spartan, the simplest Chevy available, with few adornments. They did not waste and squander.

But here is the heart of my long reverie; Grandpa built from material gathered here and there because of economic necessity.

God knows nothing of economic necessity. His resources are unlimited. He never lacks. He never sleeps. He is never confused or perplexed. He is never in need. He is never worried. But He is a builder. He created the world out of nothing.

Shortly thereafter sin fouled his beautiful creation and tarnished the reflection of His image in mankind and throughout His creation, but before the foundation of the world he had in his heart a blueprint of redemption—a rebuilding strategy. He who created the worlds with His words gathers the scraps of fallen humanity and re-builds.

Don't miss this and never doubt it. God builds beautiful things with material He gathers from the ruins of our lives. This is good news, the best of news for us, who are capable of devastating ruin. So here is an encouraging word if you ever find yourself sitting among the ruins of your life:

> *"The Spirit of the Lord GOD is upon Me, Because the LORD has anointed Me To preach good tidings to the poor; He has sent Me to heal the brokenhearted, To proclaim liberty to the captives, And the opening of the prison to those who are bound; [2] To proclaim the acceptable year of the LORD, And the day of vengeance of our God; To comfort all who mourn, [3] To console those who mourn in Zion, To give them beauty for ashes, The oil of joy for mourning, The garment of praise for the spirit of heaviness; That they may be called trees of righteousness, The planting of the LORD, that He may be glorified." [4] And they shall rebuild the old ruins, They shall raise up the former desolations, And they shall repair the ruined cities, The desolations of many generations.* (NKJV Isaiah 61:1-4)

His ability to redeem and rebuild is infinite. He is not limited by time. His intent to restore and rebuild can leap across generations of brokenness, captivity, bondage, and mourning. That's just the way He is. You have His word on that.

Chapter 11
GOD OF THE FALLEN SPARROW

Grandpa was a farmer and a machinist and, in his mid-fifties he was ordained to the gospel ministry. He worked a full-time job, farmed in the evenings and on Saturdays, and conducted prayer meeting at Linnville Church every Wednesday night and Sunday School and church every Lord's Day. He and Grandma would often have dinner in Newark at a restaurant on Wednesday night on the way out to Prayer Meeting. On the Lord's Day they almost always had a steak at "The Ponderosa" before going home to feed the cows and nap. No matter how crowded his schedule the people expected their pastor to feed them every week and they didn't go hungry.

I can see him with his glasses and his Bible and his books and reference material and his old, black manual typewriter. He used every tiny bit of margin to type his messages. He left a briefcase full of them with us when he went to be with the Lord.

Full-time pastors commonly struggle to find time for preparation. For bi-vocational pastors it is even more difficult. One Saturday morning Grandpa was in the milk house with a lot on his mind. His faith was at low ebb.

Times were tough and things were thin and he was feeling low. Bills were due and things around the farm were in need of repair. He sat milking his cow and wondering what he had to say to the people that would gather for worship the next day. Quietly he began to talk out loud to the Lord, rolling the burdens of his heart over on the Lord in prayer.

While he was praying he heard a "thump." Just a few days before he had replaced a window in the milk house. Sparrows had been getting into the milk house and making a mess. They were used to flying through the open window. He walked outside to see that a little sparrow had flown into the new glass and it had fallen to the ground. He stood looking at the little bird for a while. Relief from his discouragement and text for a message flowed into his heart.

The words of the text were the words of Jesus recorded in Matthew 10:29-31 "Are not two sparrows sold for a copper coin? And not one of them falls to the ground apart from your Father's will. But the very hairs of your head are all numbered. Do not fear therefore; you are of more value than many sparrows."

Looking at the fallen sparrow and thinking of the word of Jesus, it was as if the sun burned through the clouds of his soul. The God who numbers the hairs of our heads and notices the fallen sparrow would provide, and that is something worth reminding the people who would gather in the morning in the little church on Route 40.

I heard him tell this story from the pulpit of his church in Linnville, Ohio. It is one of the few places all three of us who share the name Kenneth Pierpont have preached.

Grandfather died in October of 1980. Grandma lived another twenty some years. On the day of her funeral I overheard my Dad and Uncle Bill talking. They were talking about my Grandmother's estate. Because of Grandpa's hard work, Grandma's modest, frugal living, and the provision of God, they had all they needed until the day both of them went to the place where there is no more need.

They trusted the God of the fallen sparrow, and spoke of Him all of their lives to all who would listen. I hope you will, too.

Chapter 12
A SURPRISE IN THE DRIVEWAY

When I was small, before my Grandfather Pierpont had retired from Owens Corning Fiberglass in Newark, we visited the farm one weekend. It was in those first few warm and wonderful days of summer. We suburban kids longed so deeply to feel the grass between our toes. We longed for the touch of the evening breeze on our face, the sun on our heads, the scent of things that grow. We longed for a ride on the tractor - for an evening with our cane poles on the edge of the quiet pond as the summer evening set in and the sound of the crickets' crescendo with the waning light.

When we arrived Grandpa announced that he had a surprise for us. It was in the lane. We would have to search for it. We all scurried to see what it was. The factory had discarded dozens of large green balls that looked like dark green glass marbles a little darker in color than telephone insulator glass, but similar. Each round glass ball had a certain imperfection in it. Grandpa had spread them in the drive and told us if we found them we could have them. We gathered them like greedy, little pirates.

Back home marbles this size were called "boulders" and we discovered to our delight that they were coveted by the neighbor kids. I had a large supply of them at one time so I swapped them for "steelies" and for other "boulders," and sometimes for baseball cards.

Grandma and Grandpa survived the depression, but not without hunger and not without hardship and not without watching my great grandfather lose my grandfather's childhood home–a pleasant farm whose house crowned a hill, looking out over hills and valleys of pasture and field. It was on the main road through Chatham just north of town so we often reversed the sad story. I think it must have been a part of who my grandparents were.

Grandma and Grandpa were serious about their work. They were diligent about their savings. They were conscientious about the smallest expenditure. They didn't waste things. They didn't throw away things that were used. They salvaged and found multiple uses for things. They saved things others threw away. They saw value in things others had no use for. Grandpa immediately saw value in the unique green glass balls.

That was years ago. The farm is no longer in the family. The place is still there but almost nothing survives now that I remember from my youth except for the great spruce still standing on the bank of the spring run. You could sift every stone in the lane that winds down from the road over the creek to the house and you would find nothing but white native limestone gravel. I'm sure over the years we mined every green glass ball from that lane. I would very much love to have one of those marbles today. A stranger would never understand their value, but if you were to show one to my brothers or my sister I'm sure it would start a bidding war.

What if we had the ability to see today the value something would have once the years have passed? What if we could see ahead and know how worthless some things are that preoccupy us and worry us now? Wouldn't it be good to be able to see things that way?

I pray that God will help me see the value of things the way he sees them—through the lens of His perfect, eternal evaluation. When time is no more what will I value, what will I cherish? What among the things that I worry about here will lose its value when time is no more? Are you sure what you are worrying about right now is worth worrying about? Are you sure the things you squander now won't have value one day?

Chapter 13
UGLY WEEDS

Most of my memories of the farm in Licking County
are pleasant, bordering on romantic. But no matter how
much time passes there is one memory that is impossible
to romanticize. It is the memory of a chore I am still
convinced my grandfather thought up just to burn off my
excess energy and keep me out of trouble.

Before they invented video games parents had to be
more creative. On a summer afternoon when I needed
something to keep myself occupied, I didn't have a room
full of electronic gizmos. Back then I could never have
conceived of the Internet, Facebook, iPods, VCRs, DVDs,
or cable TV. Grandpa was born before radios, cars,
manned air flight, moon landings or space travel, let alone
cyberspace. They were just getting over the novelty of radio
when TV swept America. For a long time we didn't have a
TV and when we did it was a small black and white set for
years.

My grandfather would sometimes give me a "weed
whip" and tell me to walk along the road and cut down
what he called Canadian thistles. That was not only before
video games, it was before they invented gas-powered

weed-eaters. The tool was similar to a golf club and it was not gas or electric powered. It was boy-powered—hot, sweating, in-the-direct-August-afternoon-sun-boy-powered. In the oppressive heat I struggled against fears of infected blisters, heat-stroke, dehydration and death. I imagined my grandfather's great guilt-induced grief at my funeral. My younger brother Kevin would have the room all to himself. He would probably sell my bike, starve my dog, drown my white mice and take over the top bunk. Kevin was really a great kid, but heat has a way of playing tricks with your mind.

Chopping down Canada thistles was only temporarily effective because if you didn't pull them out by the roots and runners they would grow again. Grandpa wanted to cut them down before they could blossom into purple flower and go to seed. The seeds would blow around the farm and the pests would multiply. He also knew it was a good idea to do something to channel my boundless energy into something at least mildly productive.

If you do a little research you will see that Canada thistles are a terrible scourge to North American grain farmers. They grow fast and tall, quickly reaching over five feet in height. The United States and Canadian governments have spent millions of dollars without success to try to find a way to eradicate this aggressive weed. Butterflies and birds love it, but it is very costly to farmers so they have good reason to hate it. You can't let weeds like that take over the farm any more than you can let restless boys wander around without productive things to do or you are asking for trouble—but that is another story—actually a series of harrowing tales I promise to tell you another day.

Have you seen the "Life is good" line of clothing? This little "Life is good" mascot Jake wears a perpetual smile and poses by the crackling fire, or paddles a kayak, or rides his bike, or runs, climbs mountains, eschews television, and just plain loves life. Jake's life is good. I love the idea, even it is only true in a qualified way. I have a few "Life is good" shirts and even a "Life is good" sticker on my Jeep, but the slogan is only really true in a qualified way. Life is good, as is all that God has created, but something is terribly wrong and badly broken. Optimism ends where the curse begins.

The whole sad story is told in Genesis:

Then to Adam He said, "Because you have heeded the voice of your wife, and have eaten from the tree of which I commanded you, saying, 'You shall not eat of it': "Cursed is the ground for your sake; In toil you shall eat of it All the days of your life. Both thorns and thistles it shall bring forth for you, And you shall eat the herb of the field. In the sweat of your face you shall eat bread Till you return to the ground, For out of it you were taken; For dust you are, And to dust you shall return."
(NKJV Genesis 3:17-19)

As beautiful as this earth is, it's not all flowers and bird songs. Every day isn't sunny and delightful. Little furry creatures commonly grow up to eat each other. According to the most reliable of sources (the eighth chapter of Romans) the earth is groaning under a curse and has been since the Garden of Eden when sin first crashed the party. That really does explain a lot. Because the earth is full of the glory of the Lord but a lot of really bad things happen on God's earth every day.

God's creation is beautiful beyond belief and you and I are a part of God's creation—the pinnacle of God's creation. But because of sin, creation is fallen and groaning and we all groan along with it. We groan for a time when the curse will be reversed—for a time when the earth will be redeemed, renewed, reborn, and restored, delivered from the bondage of corruption. We groan with it, because we are a part of creation and we suffer the effects of the fall and the curse. Paul wrote; "...we groan within ourselves eagerly waiting for the adoption, the redemption or our body..." The Spirit also groans making intercession for us.

I am a "glass half-full kind of guy" and sometimes people will question the appropriateness of my optimism. They have good cause to do so—the curse on creation. Everything isn't rosy. Something really is desperately wrong. It's not always a balmy summer evening. The stars are not always visible high in the dome of heaven. People hurt people. Some suffer innocently. Children are abused and neglected. Poor are oppressed. Injustice and depravity abound. The evening breeze does not always bear the fragrance of living things. Sometimes we are overcome with the toxic fumes of dying things. As long as we are in this sin-cursed word there will be weeds to whack and thorns and roses will grow together. The little one-in-a-million snowflakes will sometimes gather in angry anarchy and wipe out the idyllic alpine village in a violent avalanche.

But it will not always be that way. There will be a regeneration some day. A time of restoration to life. Jesus will reign there forever. The New Jerusalem will come down out of heaven one day and there will be a New Heaven and a New Earth. (Revelation 21:1-3) Peter said it this way. *"...according to His promise, look for new heavens and a new earth in which righteousness dwells."* (NKJV 2 Peter 3:13)

Creation is awesome and you are a part of that. Creation is fallen and you are a part of that, too. One day creation will be redeemed and you can be a part of that by the grace of God and the atoning work of the Lord Jesus Christ.

One day in the new earth I am going back to revisit the hill farm in Licking County to see what God has done with the little spot on earth that was so dear to me as a boy —my heartland. I will smell the new mown hay on the moist evening air. I will lie at night and gaze out into God's heaven. I will eat again of the good produce of the earth but, mercifully, there will be no weeds to whack.

Chapter 14
POP THE CLUTCH

Grandpa owned a "back-up" tractor. It was a little gray
Massey-Furgeson, the forerunner to the popular Ford 8N,
I think. I don't have all the details, but Grandpa was pretty
sure that Henry Ford stole the hitch design from Harry
Ferguson. I did a little research and found out that
Ferguson won a ten-million-dollar suit over it, so I don't
feel too bad for him. Ten million dollars was a lot of
money back then. (Even today I think I could get by nicely
for two or three years on that much money). The tractors
were all manufactured in Michigan, made in Dearborn,
just a few miles from here but to me they seemed as
indigenous to central Ohio as dogwoods in spring.

If I was ever tempted to restore a piece of equipment it
would be one of these historic tractors. In my study I have
a tiny replica of one. Whenever I see one it floods my heart
with warm memories. I can smell the grease and the new-
mown hay. I can hear the distinct sputter of the engine. I
can remember the clear blue June sky and the pure
sweetness of riding up the lane on the tow-bar with my
hands on the fenders watching the clover pass under the
wheels and talking to Grandpa.

I don't know why but it never had a starter the whole time I worked with my grandfather. If it stalled in the field you would have to get another tractor, hook it up to a log chain, and pull it to jump-start it. In the evening he parked it on a bank out behind the barn and in the morning you would just hop on, turn the ignition to "on" put it in neutral, put in the clutch and release the brake. When the little gray machine gained speed on the hill you would pop the clutch and the thing would sputter to life.

I always thought it would be a good idea to just buy a new starter, but by the late 70's those were probably pretty hard to come by, I suppose. The old tractor ran just fine if you knew how to get it started. For a while in college I had to use the same technique to get my VW started. If it stalled I would get out and run along side with the door open pushing it, jump in, turn the ignition, depress the clutch, put it in gear, and quickly release the clutch (which for some reason we called "popping" the clutch). The car would start or I would have to tie up traffic until it did. A lot of the things I learned on the farm have been useful for years.

In 1990 we lived in Mt. Vernon, Ohio on West Gambier Road. It was a very nice part of town, but it was town. The boys wanted to live in the country. We all did. Over breakfast at McDonald's one morning our oldest son Kyle asked, "Dad, can we live in the country?"

I said; "Well, son if you want to live in the country, ask the Lord for a place in the country. If he wants us to live in the country, he can arrange it. If not we can assume the Lord wants us to stay where we are." He and his brother began to pray every night that we would find a place to live in the country.

Not two weeks later we drove out to the farm on Rutledge Road for the first time. We lived for almost four of our family's wonderful growing-up years on that old farm in a valley in pleasant Ohio. The property was in a flood-plain so our place was alone in the valley and always would be.

During those years my study was in an upstairs garret room under the west-facing gable of the house. I surrounded myself there with my treasured books. The books rested on stout shelves built from old concrete forms as a labor of love by my loyal friend Gary Mickle. My desk was a huge green Steelcase monster given to me early in my pastoral ministry. It was a modest study, but I doubt if I will ever have a better place to write.

The view from the casement window of my room looked out across a few acres of corn to a lovely wood. Hidden a few dozen yards into the wood a creek gurgled toward the river. There the children and the dogs played. Along the creek was a bank of mint, fragrant when I would mow it off with the brush hog.

The farm came equipped with a Farmall "H" tractor. The "H" was dangerous on the hills especially with a novice like me at the wheel. One day I mowed over an oil line with it, to the amusement of some workers who happened to be looking on.

At the corner of the house was a Chinese elm, host to the most wonderful homemade swing any of us have ever experienced. To think of that swing now after the passing of years and the little girl in it, blonde hair blowing in the wind is a memory almost too rich to take.

I loved to start the day by climbing the steep ridge that ran along the north-west section of the property. Among a symphony of birdsong I would read my testament and spend time with the Lord. From the hillside I could look down on the house and barns situated in the valley and the road snaking away into the distance.

In back was a huge yard big enough to hit fly-balls to the boys and fly kites in the spring. It was big enough for our Thanksgiving Day football games and summer camp-outs complete with campfires. We bought the boys good air-rifles and they scouted the farm like Daniel Boone and Davy Crockett from early morning until it was too late to see.

It was there our little beagle, Yoder, lived a few happy months and died. He was run over by a truck, one of the rare visitors to the farm. He is buried on the bank of the creek there. Thereafter and to this day we renamed the creek "Yoder Creek" a memorial to our little hound. It was to the Rutledge Road farm we brought our Golden Retriever puppy, Ginger. She roamed the farm, terrorized groundhogs and rabbits, and reigned as its unrivaled queen. We had a few cats there, too and a few unwanted critters indoors that my wife doesn't want me to tell about.

On Rutledge Road I took walks with the children and the dog whenever there was a full moon. Sometimes we walked under the canopy of trees a mile or more back to the river. We followed an old roadbed that had been out of use for seventy years since the bridge spanning the river washed out and was never replaced. The old roadbed was covered over with a carpet of grass.

Our bedroom was on the first level surrounded by a screen porch. On a summer night we could open two doors that led to the porch and enjoy the sound of crickets, the cool breeze, and the fragrance of the night. Our sixth child, Daniel was born in that bedroom on a night in early November under a rare occurrence of the Aurora Borealis.

The front yard was shaded by a maple that flamed brilliant red in the fall and shed its leaves in a crimson carpet around my chair. I loved to read in that chair, an Adirondack I bought cheap from an old fiddler we met at a street fair.

When we moved to the farm I noticed the small enclosed back porch needed some attention. One autumn afternoon I was looking for a chore that would justify about three hours of listening to football on the radio. I settled on painting the back porch. I painted the porch bright white. On the porch was a board with a row of pegs to hang chore coats. There was a shelf. I kept my bird books there with binoculars and a decorative bluebird house. Under the shelf I arranged a bench so you could sit down there and pull your boots off after a walk. When I was done with that porch it was one of my favorite rooms in the house. I kept my walking stick there on a peg hanging from a leather strap. It was my exploring companion.

A friend gave us a bent canoe and we floated it down the Kokosing River. We did just a little fishing but it was too ugly to describe here and we are not proud of it. That was before we discovered the art of fly-fishing.

The property came complete with its own gas well. We had no heating expense. We sometimes regulated the heat in the dead of winter by simply opening the door for a while. The well water was sweet as spring water.

We discovered an old toboggan in a shed and foolishly hauled it to the top of a hill across the road from the house, loaded it with the whole family, and pushed off. We flew down the hill gaining speed as we went, out of control. The huge sled leaped the ditch, crossed the road, and came to rest against a huge pine. No one wanted to ride again. We once rode runner sleds down the steep run under the power lines down the steepest part of the hill digging in with our feet to keep under control. When we lost control it was reminiscent of the "agony-of-defeat" crash scene in the introduction to the Wide World of Sports television broadcast.

I risked my life one frigid night to climb up into the dark peak of the barn to hang a star of lights. We wanted everyone for miles to know of our loyalty to Christ and our joy at the celebration of his nativity. We secured a memory none of us who saw it will ever erase from our minds.

In the winter I would walk out in the night crunching snow and look back on the house sheltering the people I loved most in the world. From within glowed the lone light in the valley. On nights like that I thought I could spend the rest of my life on the farm on Rutledge Road but our landlord died in a tractor accident and his widow needed to sell the place. Our time in the valley was done.

Our time on Rutledge Road was a kindness from the hand or our good Lord. We spent some of our happiest years and gathered some of our sweetest memories there, and it was an answer to a nine-year-old boy's prayer.

When we got out to the farm for the first time the owner showed us around. He bragged on the well water and the features and benefits of the place. He walked out to the barn and pulled the door open to reveal a beautiful little gray Ford 8N that could have been the very tractor on the old farm. It had it's own starter and it ran like a top.

When I got on the little 8N it would take me back in time. The tractor and the smell of the dust and grease and feed and hay in the barn reminded me of all that I loved about the weeks in the summer and the weekends I spent on my grandfather's farm.

In fifty years of life and over thirty years of pastoral ministry I have noticed that people all have their own unique motivational patterns. To get the best out of them you have to know just how they work. I want to inspire and encourage the ones I love. I want to be there for them to help them be their best. I want to be a lifelong member of their fan-club. I know I have to be a student of the people in order to influence them to be at their best.

I want to be an expert at every one of my kids. I want to make a life-long study of my wife. The Bible says; "...live with your wife according to knowledge..." If you are a husband you need to know your wife better than you knew the owner's manual of your 1964 GTO. If you are a wife, you want to be the woman who knows him best. That should keep you busy for a lifetime. If someone you love is ever overcome with the hardships of life, you want to know what needs to be done to get them up and running again.

Chapter 15
BUS RIDE HOME

Some of my memories are stories. They have plot and setting and character. Some of them are just snapshots or videos that I cherish in the archive of my memory.

In one of them gravel roads girdled the gentle hills of rural Licking County. I am riding the bright yellow school bus that growls along them one fall afternoon. It is comfortably cool. The sun is going down the crisp blue, October sky. From my seat in the bus I watch the fields and forests pass. Wind stirs golden fields of corn drying for harvest. Bright sunlight glistens off blue farm ponds. Red and yellow maples stir up a love of and longing for beauty in me that has never been fully satisfied.

The bus rounds the top of the hill by the split rail fence on the Western edge of the farm and then gears down and stops in the road across the spring run and up the hill from the house. The door opens and I step down and walk across the road and into the yard where my little brothers wait with a football. We play in the fallen maple leaves until the sun touches the tops of the trees, the sky blushes toward dusk, and they call us in for supper. It is an ordinary autumn afternoon that, for some reason, is captured on the film of my mind and stored in the archive of my memory. I can play it again on demand.

I always wonder what moments will be burned onto the film of my children's minds and stored in the archive of their memories. I pray they will be happy, healthy ones that tug them toward God and remind them of how much we love them. I find myself praying:

Merciful God; Help me guard my tongue, my time, and my temperament with my loved ones so the roots of their souls will grow down into the healthy soil of sweet memories. Without your help I know that my sinful flesh would destroy the people I love. Work in me God, and quickly, before the sun sets in autumn and all my memories are made. –Amen

Chapter 16
A THOUSAND SACRED SWEETS

To follow the Crucified One will always involve some suffering. He was the Man of Sorrows, and called men to take up their cross if they were going to follow Him. But Jesus was also anointed with the oil of gladness above all of his fellows.

As beautiful as eternity will be God daily loads us with benefits throughout our earthly lives. One of the joys of life is to discover the delightful things that God has poured bountifully out on the earth. There are times we are expected to fast as an act of worship, but there are also times He commands His people to feast as an act of worship. There is great fulfillment and joy in following Jesus, here and now, not just in eternity. The Christian life is not intended to be a life of stoic self-denial and self-inflicted suffering.

There was a slope of hay field toward the North end of my grandpa's wonderful little farm. In the evening it was shaded by a woods. In the afternoon it was warm and bright with sunlight. It was on top of the hill, well out of sight of the house. From that spot there were no houses or man-made structures in view. It was a pleasant, peaceful place.

One afternoon I was with grandpa while he was working the field and he said; "Why don't you go over there against the woods and see what you see in the grass." As was so often the case, I didn't see anything. As was usually the case he told me to look again. I did. I still didn't see anything.

Finally he shut down the equipment and climbed to the ground. He walked over and pointed down. I looked. It looked like weeds to me. He bent over and picked up something that was between white and pale pink. He handed it to me.

"Try this and tell me what you think."

I put it in my mouth. "Strawberry. It's good," I said.

"They're wild strawberries. They grow here every year."

On a summer afternoon when I had time to explore I would hike up the the upper field over against the woods and lay on my stomach and eat the little strawberries in the afternoon. It is a happy boyhood memory.

Years later on a day-off trip as a family we were exploring the backroads of the Ohio Amish Country in Holmes County, north of Licking County. It was toward the fall of the year. The Mennonites were holding a revival service in a huge tent. We decided we would attend the revival that evening. Late in the afternoon a thunderstorm rolled through the area, knocked out power and blew the tent down. They moved the revival service to a local church for the evening. There was no power so there were no instruments and no microphones.

Even without the aid of electronics the music was beautiful. There must have been over five hundred mostly Amish and Mennonite people in attendance and they were used to singing a cappella. One of the songs they sang that night was "We're Marching to Zion." I've never forgotten that night and the beauty of that song. When I heard it my mind went back to that happy simple memory of a summer afternoon with my grandfather. Here's the verse that sent me back to my boyhood on the farm:

The hill of Zion yields a thousand sacred sweets
Before we reach the heavenly fields
Before we reach the heavenly fields
Or walk the golden streets
Or walk the golden street

For those whose faith is in Jesus our destination will be unspeakably beautiful and God has arranged a delightful trip for us too.

When the children were small we learned to sing "We're Marching to Zion" a cappella as a family and sang it in conferences and churches. Today when I hear it I remember those times and my mind goes back to our Monday trips when the children were all small and lived at home and farther back to the sweetness of the hillside farm.

Chapter 17
HEART FOOD

Everyone has their heartland and everyone has their heart food. The hills of central Ohio will always be in my heart and my heart food comes from the animals that grazed and the vegetables that grew there. Beef, potatoes (preferably mashed and drowned with butter and brown gravy), corn, tomatoes, real, authentic green beans popping out of their dark green pods, limas, carrots, and blackberry pie are my heart food. I can tolerate Chinese food. I enjoy Mexican, Cajun, Italian, and Greek food. But it is food from my heartland that puts a lump in my throat and a tear in my eye like standing on a Memorial Day on the streets of Utica, Ohio and watching Old Glory pass down the street borne by a band of patriotic old brothers from the VFW.

The farm was a working farm. Grandpa raised white-faced Hereford beef cattle. He raised hay and corn for the cattle. As a result there was always plenty of good, farm-raised beef. On Sunday Grandma and Grandpa loved to stop at the restaurant they liked to call "The Ponderosa" in Newark for a steak and baked potato with sour cream and butter.

Sometimes we had Sunday dinner at the farm. When we arrived home in winter months we would feed the cattle. We would take a few bales of hay out to the dormant winter pasture and cut the twine over the side of the wagon. Then we would go back to house and Grandma would have roast with carrots, and potatoes ready for us.

When Grandma put a platter of roast beef on the table for Sunday dinner I wanted to stand at attention and put my hand over my heart. It's that good. BD's Mongolian barbecue is a tasty novelty, but it's not the kind of thing my Grandma would understand. I would drop my chopsticks in a heartbeat for a piece of pumpkin pie, even if I did have to wash it down with Grandma's industrial waste coffee.

Grandma and Grandpa could grow cabbage, too. Grandma had a recipe for vegetable stew that combined almost everything that farm boys in central Ohio love to eat; carrots, potatoes, green beans, peas, limas, cabbage and chunks of lean beef. She would make huge vats of it and can it to eat all winter long. It was good immediately but after the whole thing stewed together the flavor tasted like Bluegrass harmony. It just sang. It was folk music for the tummy. I pity kids who have to try to hang on to life eating Taco Bell and Burger King. It's just sad.

Chapter 18
HELPING WITH THE HARVEST

Holmes County, Ohio is Ohio Amish Country. It is beautiful any time of the year, but it is especially beautiful at harvest time. Harvest is hard work for any farm family, but it is especially intense for Amish farmers who do not use modern farm equipment. David Kline is an Amish farmer with a large family, but even with a large family there is enough work at harvest time to exhaust everyone and the dairy cows still have to be milked before daylight even during harvest time.

Amish men don't have televisions, radios, computers or cell phones so they have time to tell stories. David Kline has an unusual story-telling gift. David Kline writes his stories down and he publishes them, and people read them—lots of people. His stories are well-written, published, and poplar. David Kline has stories to tell. In his first book, *Great Possessions*, he tells this story about harvest time.

On Amish farms in Ohio the main meal is dinner, at noon. The Amish eat well at every meal but supper is modest. At supper David told his family; "We are all going to have to pull together this evening and get the rye harvest in (shock the rye) before we go to bed no matter how long it takes. Even if we have to work into the night we can't afford to risk losing the rye if it rains tonight. We have to work as long as it takes to get it off."

The whole family went to work right after dinner working their way methodically up through the field toward the crest of the hill. The hill was halfway to the neighboring farm. They worked slowly but steadily. They knew they would be half-done when they reached the top of the hill.

The sun sank lower and lower toward the dark line in the west as they worked. Approaching the crest of the hill they heard voices on the other side. When they crested the hill they were delighted to see that the neighbors had taken initiative to help them with their harvest. All down the hill toward the neighbor's farm the rye stood in shocks row on row. The work was done before the sun sank from sight. Thinking they were halfway done suddenly the job was over.

They stood at the crest of the hill for a while and looked with satisfaction on the results of their mutual labor, then agreed to join their families together for one more task before nightfall, the task of making homemade ice cream. As a day of harvesting came to an end the families had plenty of time to laugh at the antics of the children, tell stories, and enjoy the sweetness of homemade ice cream and the fellowship of good neighbors – the kind that don't have to be told when their help is needed.

When Jesus said, "The fields are ripe unto harvest," He was talking about people. If you look around there are people everywhere you look who need to be brought in before it's too late and that is more likely to happen if we can discover ways to work together. Build teams. Appreciate the skills and gifts of others. When you see someone needs help, pitch in. Try to cooperate when you can. Put pettiness aside. And then someday at sunset we will all sit down and enjoy the sweetness of our labor.

Chapter 19
HARVEST MOON

On the farm when harvest-time came Grandpa would piece together his old one-row corn picker and oil it up for the season. It had seen many seasons. He pulled it behind a little Ford 8N tractor and hooked a wagon on the back of the corn-picker. It was a noisy contraption unlike these huge modern green monsters you see shaving the grain off wide, flat fields in wide gulps these days.

His whole operation was like that. Basic. His life was like that, too. He worked hard, helped others and you could count on him to keep his promises. That's what made it so hard one autumn when time and responsibilities and difficult circumstances closed in on him. He needed to harvest a few acres of his own corn. He also promised to harvest a few ribbons of corn that wound around the hills on a friend's farm, too. Problems came. First equipment trouble. Usually he was able to fabricate something or rig the equipment so the job could be done but after he had harvested his own corn his little corn picker coughed, sputtered and quit. It was out of use until a special part came from distant lands and that would be too late to help this year. Then the equipment problem was followed by a time problem. The factory had orders to fill and began to require overtime. He was leaving the farm before light and arriving home after dark.

He sat at the kitchen table and nursed a cup of awful coffee while he wondered aloud what to do. Grandma said that there was simply nothing he could do. He would have to tell his friend that he couldn't help with his corn. He mused on it and considered his options. The idea of asking his friend to release him from his promise didn't sit well with him. His friend was depending on him. "If you don't have the equipment, you just can't do it," his wife said. "Well, I could do it the way we used to do it. I could harvest it by hand." "You don't have time to do that with the overtime, besides it would be dark."

He consulted the Farmer's Almanac. Late in October there would be another full moon. It is called the harvest moon because it gives farmers more light and increases their harvest time.

"If the Lord gives us clear weather, I think I can do it," he said.

And he did. The weather was cold and clear and the moon was brilliant. After work he made his way to the field and his wife met him with dinner and a thermos of more of the awful, strong, black coffee. Then he worked through the night to keep his word.

I'm proud to have the same name as he did. I've spent hours on the fender of the tractor with my grandpa. I've even suffered through some of that same awful coffee. But I had never heard about this incident until I was having a talk with my grandmother one day about values she and Grandpa believed very deeply in—hard work and keeping your promises.

My grandpa did work hard and keep his promises. He also loved his family. I am proud to have his name. Sometimes, when I am tempted to cut corners or defer responsibilities, I think of my grandfather out under the harvest moon bending low and swinging his sharp corn-knife in a wide arch. I can hear the thump of ears of corn hitting the floor of the wagon and the music of geese honking their way across the cold October sky against the brilliance of the harvest moon.

In the dark early hours of the morning, when his work was done, he crawled his tired body up into the seat of the old tractor and made his way home. Behind him in the pale moonlight, I can see row after row of corn shocks standing at attention in respect for a man who keeps his word.

One day I received an e-mail from Ray Reiman who grew up on a farm in Iowa. He read this story and here is what he had to say:

> *Great story about your granddad harvesting corn! He was much like my dad—a hard working, very honest farmer who died some years ago at age 89. Dad also was a fantastic corn "picker" by hand—not necessarily before*

one-row pickers were used but before he had money to buy such a fancy machine.

Even though Dad was much older than we highschool sons on our Northwest Iowa farm, he could out-pick any two of us! And he did! As my oldest brother and I were picking corn at one wagon behind him, we had a heck of a time keeping up with him!

Of course, our wagons were each "powered" by a team of horses that we harnessed in the dark (after first feeding the hogs, milking the cows and eating breakfast!) and drove to the field before daylight. I remember having to first "find" the ears of corn in the darkness to pitch into the wagon.

After each filling our wagons by throwing the ears against the "bang boards" by noon, we'd head home to unload the corn at the elevator at the corn crib, feed the horses, eat a quick lunch ("dinner" in those days), and head back to the field to start the whole business once again.

By the time it got too dark to pick any more, we'd drive back home to unload the corn into the corn crib, unharness and feed the horses, cattle and hogs, eat supper, drag our tired bodies into bed for a night's sleep to start all over again before daylight the next day!!!

Oh, by the way, when we were younger, this all started with a two-week "vacation" (yeah, right!) from GRADE school that was declared every fall so that we kids could help pick corn!!!

Then, as we got into highschool and beyond, Dad would let us use his horses and wagons to pick corn for larger-farm neighbors so we could go out and make big bucks! Hey, as much as 3c-5c a bushel at first and then later as awesome as 10c a bushel! And if we were good, we could make as much as $10 a day!

Wow! And kids think they have it tough these days! I don't think we ever complained. We certainly never even thought of not going out to pick corn every day!...
...It's been fun reminiscing, Ken! Thanks for listening!

—Ray

One of the last conversations I had with my grandmother was early in the morning after I had worked through the wee hours of the early morning loading UPS trucks. I was tired and sweaty from the hard work and early-rising. I was trying to start a church and provide for our family. I was only a few blocks from the little house where Grandma lived in Newark, so I stopped in for a visit, even though I was very tired.

She was glad to see me. I told her I was tired and apologized for my appearance. I said, "Sorry about the way I look. I've been working hard."

That just put fire in her blue eyes, "Of course you are working hard. You have all those mouths to feed. You have to work hard to take care of them."

I realized that I had touched a nerve and she was expressing to me a value that was deeply embedded in her and Grandpa's life. They married at the very end of the Great Depression. They started marriage with nothing. God gave Grandpa a job at the factory when others were waiting outside warming their hands over a barrel-fire to stay warm waiting for an opportunity. If his boss was not pleased with any of the workers, he would walk him over to the window and tell them to look at the men outside.

"If you don't want to work, any of those men out there would love to have your job."

One hot summer afternoon Grandpa and I went up to the north hill where he had set out a large garden. The green beans were in and we headed up to pick them. (It always amazes me that green beans from a store-bought can and green beans grown on the sunny hillside of an Ohio farm and picked and snapped on the porch in the evening and prepared in a pressure-cooker and lovingly placed into thick glass jars and stored in the cool basement and drawn out for family meals in mid-winter can be both be called by the same name).

Grandpa gave me my assignment and went away for an hour to work on something else. When he returned I announced that I had finished the job. He frowned, walked over to the rows, bent down, and started picking beans from the row that I had already picked. To this day I can still feel the rebuke of it. Grandpa didn't understand that kind of carelessness.

Times change and values vary, but hard work and keeping your promises will never go out of style.

Chapter 20
MEETING GOD IN A CORNFIELD

When my Grandpa Pierpont was saved he was just twelve years old. It was in a revival service at the Chatham Methodist Church in Chatham, Ohio. He was even a Methodist lay preacher once when he was a boy. At the time he sensed a call to be a pastor. But some things confused him. Something made him wonder if he was really saved. There must have been some sin, some youthful lust, some worldly tug that made him doubt his salvation. It may be that his father contributed to his confusion with a little over-zealous theology. Grandpa once told me that he stole some watermelon on a hot day and at dinner that night his father confronted him and told him that he doubted if he was saved since he stole. His older brother Elmer was caught chewing tobacco and my great grandfather told him that he must not be saved because saved people don't use tobacco. In our family stories about that generation none survive that would indicate they saw the sin of anger in the same light.

I'm sure Satan was at work to confuse my grandfather. As a young man he set aside his relationship with God and began to pursue many other things. He was interested in farming, boxing, baseball, and bikes. He met a pretty blue-eyed girl at the Farmer's Market in Newark one day. She was eight years younger than he. She was a faithful church member but she was not saved. She had never really heard or clearly understood the gospel of God's grace and the truth of justification by faith, let alone the security of the believer or the perseverance of the saints.

Years later when my Dad came to Christ in the Navy the first thing he did was come home to tell his parents of Christ. Their reactions were different. Grandma was offended that the church-going of his youth was not enough for him. Grandpa had heard the gospel and knew what my dad was talking about. Tears ran down his face as he described his childhood conversion and his drift from God. It wasn't long before he was restored to Christ.

Soon thereafter the gospel dawned on my grandmother reading a tract that Dad sent home for her. Dad helped them interview pastors and they found a good church right there in Newark. The pastor, H. E. Doyle was a graduate of Moody Bible Institute. He became my grandfather's mentor and pastor. Grandma and Grandpa were soon baptized. After that they began to grow like corn in August. They had developed a strong appetite for good reading and a lifelong desire to be with God's people. Their cultural Christianity turned into a sincere pursuit of Christ and regular fellowship with the people of God. They became Sunday morning, Sunday night, and

Wednesday night faithful until they went to be with the Lord.

One fall evening soon after his salvation my grandfather was driving through the mellow Ohio countryside and God was working on his heart. He sensed that God was doing a deeper work in him. He pulled his car off the road and stood looking into the clear, starry sky. Listening to the voice of the Spirit and following the tug of his heart he made a decision.

On his finger was a ring that represented a soul-tie and a commitment that was contrary to his new desire to pursue Christ. He felt God was telling him to break that tie. He removed the ring and threw it into the field that night and never looked back. From then on his exclusive loyalty was to the local church.

In Newark today near the hospital where our daughter Heidi Grace was born is the building of First Christian Union Church. My grandfather was the chairman of the Trustees when the building was built. Years later it was in that very building where his funeral service would be held.

I believe when my grandfather was about twelve he turned his back on a life of consecration to God. That night under the stars on the margin of a corn field in the rolling hills of central Ohio he embraced the consecrated life again. It was shortly after that that my grandfather answered the call to ministry that had come many, many years before.

The letter to the Hebrews says;

For the bodies of those animals, whose blood is brought into the sanctuary by the high priest for sin, are burned outside the camp. Therefore Jesus also, that He might sanctify the people with His own blood, suffered outside the gate. Therefore let us go forth to Him, outside the camp, bearing His reproach. For here we have no continuing city, but we seek the one to come. (Hebrews 13:11-14 NKJV).

There will come a time in each of our lives, if we want to live in intimate fellowship with Christ, we will have to go "outside the camp" and bear the reproach of Christ. We will have to leave some things behind that we used to cherish. Many of our friends will no longer understand us or desire to be with us. We will have to reject religious systems that are not built on the gospel of justification by faith alone. We will want to find or form a local church and devote ourselves to it. We will have new loyalties and new interests. If we have the life of God in us we will never be satisfied with a thin veneer of religious practice and religious talk. Our loyalties and schedules will be radically reoriented with the Lord as the great magnetic pole of our affections. This happened to Grandpa and then Grandma Pierpont, and it is my daily prayer that it will happen in each of his great-grandchildren and great-great grandchildren and in their children for generations.

Grandpa was eager to make up for lost time. He was ordained to the gospel ministry at the Christian Union Campgrounds when he was 55 years old. I was there. He pastored three churches in his ministry. While he was still employed at Fiberglass he pastored the little flock at Linnville. When he retired he took the churches in Cooney and Grand Rapids, Ohio then he returned to pastor the little church in Linnville for the rest of his life.

I don't think a single recording of my grandfather exists, but we still have a briefcase full of his typewritten messages. They formed in his heart while farming his hillside farm in Licking County. He typed them out and then drove to Linnville on the Lord's Day and on Wednesday night and delivered them to his small congregation.

The trip to Linnville was scenic. From Newark they would drive south with wide fields and high hills and green vistas all around. The drive to Linnville bisected forest and river, field and wood, vales and flowers and trees.

As a child living in mostly flat suburbia, I silently wondered if Grandma and Grandpa really knew how beautiful their parish was, how blessed they were to get to drive out there week after week, prepared for worship by the beauty of the earth.

The Old National Road has a storied history. It started in Cumberland, Maryland and stretched west all the way to Vandalia, Illinois before the project ran out of funding. Today such roads have been displaced by the Interstate Highway System. The Interstate Highway System is a fast, safe, uniform, mundane way of getting where you want to go in a car. For the conveniences afforded by the highway system you have to sell a little piece of your soul and you have to pawn a chunk of your time.

In the Interstate the constant whine of tires on concrete drowns out the music of crickets in the ditch or the peepers near the pond. You will not usually be close enough to see the undulating flight of a goldfinch along the road. You won't pass beneath an ark of stately old maples along Main Street or see children playing in the yard. Out on the uniform stretch of concrete Interstate Highway you won't have to slow down behind an Amish buggy or a farmer hauling hay. You will never have to stop to watch children disembark from a bright yellow bus and kick their way through fallen leaves on a September afternoon. The bridges and restaurants and filling stations and signs all look the same. You won't usually find unique diners along the way. You will usually be insulated from any unique character and color of the communities through which you pass. The nature of the system tries to avoid passing through any place where people cluster or congregate or trade or talk or learn or love or commune because those are the kinds of things that slow us down and interfere with our getting places. If you take the

Interstate these are things you are unlikely to see. And you won't pass little white clapboard chapels with belfries and cemeteries like the one my Grandpa pastored in a wide spot along the National Highway they call Linnville.

Across the highway from the church is one of the historic National Highway mile markers. The marker features the distance to Cumberland, Maryland and Wheeling, West Virginia and the other way, to Columbus, Ohio.

Grandpa always liked to tell a joke about Irish immigrants mistaking the marker for a gravestone for a fella' named Columbus who died at whatever age the mile marker said it was to the State Capitol. It's not a story I could properly tell. It wasn't really funny. I'm fairly certain my grandpa made it up himself, but I would love to have captured the telling on a video.

The Linnville Church was on Route 40 on a section of The National Highway. The church sat on the north side of the road on a rising bank. Behind the church was the Linnville Cemetery. Beside the church for many years was a double outhouse. The side nearest the church for the ladies, the men on the far side.

Across the road, on the south side the ground fell away into a valley. At the close of Sunday services in good weather Grandpa and Grandma would stand on the steps outside the church in the sun and greet the parishioners. It was as beautiful a country setting as any country parson could have desired. I remember playing there after the services and the good, honest country smells and the sound of the bell carrying out over the valley.

Grandpa was in the ministry for sixteen years. In the years before the well was drilled and the bathrooms installed they carried their own water in a jug every Sunday. I don't know if they ever had Sunday evening services. In fact I know that for many years Grandma and Grandpa attended evening services at Maple Avenue Christian Union Church. Occasionally they would visit First Christian Union Church or Newark Baptist Temple.

On Wednesday evenings they did have Prayer Meeting. They would drive out and open up the church for the few who would attend. Once a week Grandpa would go out and do some calling in the area. Sometimes he would visit from home to home seeking people who would allow him to engage them in a conversation about the gospel. He used a simple, clear gospel presentation. He would show people a few verses from Romans in his New Testament. He was simple and direct and clear. He never wanted to obscure the gospel or confuse people about how to be saved. He was saved in the little church in Chatham as a boy but because of confusing teaching and later theological liberalism, he wasted years of his life without the assurance of his salvation and without effectively living for God.

Along those lush country roads were some who Grandpa led to Christ. If they had children at home they would not often stay in the Linnville Church, but they would usually find a church in town that offered a full schedule of programs. Many, many years later I would run into people around Newark who were saved or influenced for Christ through my grandfather's simple, brief ministry.

I hope you will hear of me someday what I heard of him one evening in a church in Newark, "I knew your grandpa. He led me to Christ."

Chapter 21
DOLLY AND SKIPPY

Two dogs lived on the farm for most of the years that I remember, Dolly and Skippy. Skippy was colored like a beagle but she had long legs and was about the size of a golden retriever. She was a sturdy, affable farm-dog. She lay on the porch when Grandpa was home. She followed him to the field when he was farming. When he was gone she ran rabbits and killed groundhogs. She was patient with children and she knew when to stay out of Dolly's way.

Dolly's name did not adequately describe her rugged character. On winter nights she would contentedly burrow down into a snowbank and "drift" off to sleep. In the morning Grandpa would step out on the back porch and whistle. She would rise from her sleep, shake the snow off her coat and bound for the house.

Grandpa had a fanciful imagination and he had read all the Jack London stories. Maybe that's why he told me that he was pretty sure she was part wolf. I believed him for at last three reasons; I was young and vulnerable, I admired my grandfather, he knew how to "put a story over," and even a kid could tell Dolly had a wild side. She could have been a character in a Jack London story herself.

Those dogs were never in the house, they didn't have a pedigree, but they were well-fed, they were loved, and they served a purpose on the farm. They managed the ground hog population. They announced the arrival of guests and warned unwanted intruders. They added life to the place. They lived simple and happy and they both died in a contented old age right there on the modest farm where they lived their lives.

They never did a dog-show, pulled a dog-sled, or attended obedience school. They were never house-broke, they didn't have an invisible fence, they didn't wear sweaters. They were never penned up or chained and neither of them ever wore a lead. Even without formal training they had common dog-sense. If Grandpa and Grandma left for a weekend visit or vacation they didn't hire a kennel. Skippy and Dolly just kept an eye on things and looked after themselves. They were just garden-variety, farm dogs.

Sometimes we can just cherish a "too-high" opinion of ourselves and while we are yearning for stardom, success, fame, fortune, promotion, and notoriety we are wasting our precious life and squandering the simple joys all around us every day. I don't know about you but I imagine myself as a "farm dog" kind of guy.

I don't mind staying around home. I'm happy with plain food and a simple life. I like it when people take me with them on a walk but I don't mind hanging out on the porch or curling up by the fire. I'm just a little suspicious of strangers who don't smile or maybe smile too much. Fancy people are interesting but I think people like plain folk better. Plain people like Skippy and Dolly who scouted the hills of my grandpa's farm when I was a boy growing up.

> *Live in harmony with one another. Do not be haughty, but associate with the lowly. Never be conceited.* (Romans 12:16 ESV)

The farm would not have seemed like a real working farm without the dogs. They were a part of what made the farm, the farm. I don't know how else to say it. It was a humble place guarded by a couple of humble dogs and when I hear a dog tail thumping on a wooden porch I feel a warm sense of welcome.

Chapter 22
REAL TOMATOES

My cousin Di has Facebook now. When we were kids we saw each other regularly. We have our own families now and our own lives so we only see each other when someone dies, which is very sad. It was good to connect on Facebook. I scrolled through her pictures. We look a lot alike. We could pass for brother and sister. I read her interests. One of them made me smile. She has always been a bright girl, quick-witted and verbal. Even as a child she would commonly read an entire book in one day. She is a neonatal nurse practitioner so she is a competent professional, but she still has a very simple, common interest that she inherited from our grandparents like our sharp, pointed noses... she likes growing tomatoes.

Growing tomatoes has always been a big deal in our family. Like most people who survived the Great Depression, they were devoted gardeners. They grew bell peppers that Grandpa always called "mangoes." They grew wagon-loads of sweet corn. They grew wonderful green beans and cucumbers... (They always called them pickles, even though I don't remember them pickling many of them). But the memory I cherish most is the memory of garden-ripe tomatoes. They were just plain champion tomato growers. The east-facing kitchen window was always lined with big, juicy, beautiful, red tomatoes like trophies basking in the sun.

Grandpa would grab a salt shaker and sit down for lunch and eat tomatoes like apples. Our part of Ohio was perfect for perfect tomatoes. They were so common and abundant when I was growing up that I had no idea how rare and wonderful they were at the time. I long for real tomatoes to come into season.

If you bite into something that looks like a tomato and juice doesn't run down your arm, it's probably synthetic. It's not a real tomato. Real tomatoes are grown by real people in real places with real dirt and real water and real sunshine and real care and they are real good—real, real good. There really is no substitute for real tomatoes.

Zach, a man in our church, has an impressive truck-patch garden on a few acres behind his home. He and his family are very diligent people. Our son Daniel has worked for them this summer. One of the wonderful fringe benefits of his job and been occasional produce from Zach's farm. This week he came home with a beautiful basket of real, red, ripe, perfect tomatoes. Saturday we had bacon, lettuce and TOMATO sandwiches.

When I pull a burger off the grill on a warm summer evening I don't want to ruin it with a slice of insincere tomato-like product. I want a real, honest-to-goodness slice of red, ripe, juicy 'tomatoness' on that thing.

Have you noticed that there are "Christians" and then there are Christians. Sometimes you meet professing Christians who have that same "real tomato" quality of sincerity about them. You immediately get the feeling that you are with an honest, genuine, open follower of Jesus Christ. They look you in the eye. Their smile is real. Their words are sincere. They do what they say. They're honest. I hope people find me to be a "real-tomato" kind of Christian. The real thing, not some "hot-house variety" type of Christian. I don't want to be slick and professional and distant with people. I don't want to be plastic and produced. I don't want to be "canned" and full of hollow talk and clichés. I want to be the real dirt, real sun, real rain, home grown, down-to-earth and rooted in Christ kind of Christian that only the Spirit of God can produce over time.

Chapter 23
NUMBER FOUR BIRD-SHOT

Purring through the dark on a long trip one night my Dad got to talking. He told me a shocking story about our family. During the depression chickens were mysteriously disappearing from the family farm just north of Chatham, Ohio. Times were hard. Money and food were scarce.

After a number of chickens disappeared they began to realize it was not animals but humans who were spiriting the chickens away in the night.

They formed a plan. The boys took turns out on the back porch each night waiting, shotgun in hand to surprise the thieves. Late one night, long after midnight there was a noise out back. Grandpa's oldest brother, Elmer was on guard that night. Young and impulsive, he leaped up and fired the shotgun in the direction of noise. What he didn't know is that he shot a man.

This came to light a few days later when the doctor stopped by for a visit.

"Say," says Doc," Sauntering up onto the porch, "You Pierpont boys still have any of that number four birdshot?"

"Yes, some," they answered.

"I thought it might be you. That gauge isn't very common anymore. Did you have some commotion around here late Thursday night?" says Doc.

"In fact we did."

"I thought so. I dug some number four birdshot out of the Campbell boys backside the other night. I remembered you boys had some of that birdshot. Thought you might like to know."

For a while my young mind processed the shock of what my Dad just told me.

"Dad," I asked, "Do you mean that your uncle Elmer shot a man over stealing a chicken?"

"Well," Dad said, "Back then during the depression stealing chickens was a life and death matter. People depended on their gardens and livestock to sustain life."

I had an instinct that stealing chickens was not a capital offense, even during the Depression. A man's life is just worth more than a bird no matter what.

The story Dad told me made it seem like my grandfather had grown up in the Old West. Every man to himself. The survival of the fittest. My grandfather and his people were serious about their chicken.

This is probably a good time for me to remind you that there are some things about our family histories that no amount of rationalization can justify.

Can you imagine the tragedy it would have been if the neighbor boy had died of his wounds? What would it have been like to gather around in the night and realize that you had shot a hungry man to death? Wouldn't you wish for the rest of your life that you had simply shown hospitality to the neighbors and invited them over for fried chicken?

There is no justification for theft, especially the theft of the basic means of life–but neither is there justification for impetuous behavior that could cost someone their life. May future generations of Pierponts be the kind of people who are eager to feed our neighbors and slow to shoot them.

Still it is an amazing story, isn't it?

Chapter 24
THE LAST EGG

I loved to watch my grandfather eat breakfast. After the eggs and meat were gone he would butter his toast and then reach for the honey in a bottle with a narrow spout and apply the golden yellow liquid to his toast in a grid pattern with the accuracy of a draftsman. He would then use his toast to wipe his plate so perfectly clean it looked like you could put it back in the cupboard without washing it.

He said, "If you ever lived through the Great Depression you would never waste a morsel of your food ever again."

He always challenged me to see if I could win the "clean plate award" at the end of the meal. But no one could compete with Grandpa for the "clean-plate award." He always won. It was impressive.

I have an appetite for stories about food. Enduring stories often have food somewhere in them. Often at the breakfast table Grandpa would tell an old story about eating breakfast with his three brothers on the old home place on the hill north of Chatham. His favorite breakfast story was about the brothers fighting over the last egg.

The summer before his youngest brother Art died, I talked to him on the phone. It was a fascinating conversation. I took careful notes. I asked Art if he remembered the story about the last egg. Without any more prompting he launched into the story. It was exactly as my grandpa always told it.

On the farm in Chatham, where my grandfather grew up it is common to "chore" before breakfast. The boys woke up hungry but by the time the boys all gathered in after "choring," they were ravenous. The women of the house would rise early and prepare a hot breakfast while the men were out "choring." They would thunder in from the barn, hang their chore coats on pegs on the back porch and slide their chairs under the big dining room table to platters of eggs, bacon, ham, or sausage, and pancakes. It was hearty stuff for hard-working, fast-growing men.

Elmer was the oldest. Kenneth (the young man who would become my grandfather) was next in the birth order. Orville and Art were at the table with their mother and father. Art was sitting next to my grandfather. Elmer and Kenneth were sitting across from each other. Orville, the next one down in the birth-order was at the end of the table. The young men leaned in over their plates and went at the breakfast with enthusiasm, until there was only one egg left on the old platter in the center of the table.

Both Elmer and Kenneth reached for the platter at the same. They each got a firm, dairy-farmer grip on the platter and gave it a tug. For a moment the platter was suspended in mid-air as the boys tugged back and forth. The old platter must have had a crack in it. The platter split and the last egg fell. Acting quickly Orville slid us plate under the platter just in time to for the last egg to drop squarely into the middle of his plate. Elmer and Grandpa ended up each with a piece of the platter. Orville set his plate down, pinned the last egg with his fork, sliced it with his knife, and ate it while the rest of the family laughed and they all kept laughing about that story for the rest of their lives.

When you sit down to the table day after day and it is laden with food, it's good to remember where it came from. Every time you eat pause and from deep in your heart thank God for what He provided. He's been doing that for generations of our family. For millions of people all over the world food is very scarce. So we should be grateful for every piece of fruit, every fresh garden vegetable, every strip of bacon, every hotcake and every last egg.

My mother would be ashamed of me if I didn't remind you that the proper table manner in dealing with the last helping is to ask everyone else at the table if they would like anything more and if you could serve them before you eat it. That's just what civilized people do—even when they are hungry.

Chapter 25
A TALK WITH UNCLE ARTHUR

One bright Sunday morning I was making my way to the auditorium when one of the people stopped me and said, "I think you have a special visitor in the service today." I didn't think much of it. I was distracted with other things. I went up and took my place on the platform and looked out over the people. Sitting just to the left of the center aisle was a man who looked shockingly like my grandfather. When our eyes met he smiled at me enjoying my surprise.

Grandpa died in October of 1980. This was about 1988. I walked out to greet the man.

"Hello" I said extending my hand.

"Do you know who I am?" He asked.

"Well, you look like my grandpa, but he is in heaven."

"I always thought I was considerable better looking than your grandpa, but I suppose there is a resemblance. I'm your grandpa's little brother, Art."

Art was not as big a man as my grandfather, but the resemblance was unmistakable and it would go beyond the way he looked. He was a bright man with a healthy sense of humor. It was clear they were brothers. We talked for a few minutes but I had to start the service. He was traveling so I was unable to have a satisfying conversation with him afterward.

I didn't think much about him for years until one day I was working on these stories.

Art was about eight years younger than grandpa and he outlived him by at least 30 years. One day it occurred to me to call him to see if he could fill in some of the detail of the stories in this book. I reached him on the phone. He had lived for years in Beaver Dam, New York. He spent part of the year with his son-in-law and daughter in Alaska.

It was a delightful conversation.

Art told me of a time when the family had gone on the a trip and left the oldest boys, Elmer and Kenneth to watch the farm and chore. It was summer and the watermelons ripened while the family was gone. They boys wanted to do the responsible thing and they did not want the watermelon to go to waste so between the two of them they ate them all.

This resulted in unpleasant effects on their gastrointestinal system and gave them a lifelong memory.

Eating watermelon reminds me of a shadowy glimpse I had into my great grandfather's life. He was a very strict old-fashioned Methodist. From what I gather heavier on the law than the grace. Years later Grandpa would tell me that he was confused by the teaching of his youth thinking that it was his responsibility to "keep himself saved." After sincere attempts to live up to the moral standards he had been taught he came to the conclusion that he could not do it. He married Grandmother and she attended a mainline church that was enamored with the "new theology" and did not preach the gospel. This left hem in a religious fog until years later when Dad was saved and began to make the gospel clear to the family.

Art said that my grandfather was the biggest of the brothers but Elmer, who was the oldest, was the toughest. He offered that when Grandpa had been rooming with a young man who was in training to be a boxer he came home and started sparring with his older brother Elmer some. According to Art, Elmer hit him once, Grandpa went to the ground and that was their last round. I didn't believe the story and found myself wishing I could hear my grandpa's version of it. Other than this bit of fiction, Art seemed a reliable and colorful source of information about my family no one living could ever provide.

Art and I reminisced a bit about Grandpa and about his visits to the farm. He told me some of the things they did when they were young.

My memory was a little fuzzy but I seemed to remember Grandpa telling me of a friend who ran a bare wire along the length of a urinal trough in an outhouse at a Utica football game. He hooked the wire up to the battery on his Model T Ford. As I remember the story he waited until halftime when the outhouse was in full use then went out and started the car providing a shocking halftime experience for the men.

I couldn't remember if the story was a "wouldn't it be funny if" kind of story or if Grandpa told it to me as a true story. I asked Art. He said;

"Let me tell you how that happened. There was a man named Clarence McGee Hanover who owned a truck repair business in Newark. He had a problem with some of his employees. They didn't want to go out in the cold to the outhouse in the winter so they urinated in the back corner of the garage. He asked them not to but they continued to do it. He rigged a contraption like the one earlier described and hooked it up to a battery in his office. When he thought men might be transgressing he would throw the switch and send a jolt their way.

What he didn't know was that the men knew that he would often do the same thing rather than making the long trip to the outhouse in the cold. One day, when he was relieving himself one of the men went to the office and gave him a taste of his own medicine."

I'm sure Art's version was the original version for a couple of reasons. When I heard it I had the distinct feeling that I had heard it before and Art supplied specific names and details.

I will never know for sure but always believe, based on what I have learned of the Pierpont brothers that they

KEN PIERPONT

took what they learned from Clearance McGee Hanover and applied it in the incident at the Utica football game, but we will probably never know for sure. All the voices that could have told us have grown silent and while they were speaking for some reason we didn't think to ask.

I was about to end the conversation when Art said something that sounded for all the world like what I call a "story-trigger." It was something someone says when they would like to tell a story and they want you to ask them to do so.

"Ken. Sometimes truth is stranger than fiction. You know what I mean?"

"Yes."

"My son-in-law lives in Alaska, you know," he said. "I try to spend part of the year with them. One year I was going to drive from Beaver Dam, through Newark across the Western US and up the AlCan Highway to Alaska. I would make the trip in my van with my dog.

I had my tires aligned and gassed up to leave Newark at 9:40 on Wednesday morning. By 11:00 p.m. on Sunday I was in Whitehorse on the Yukon River. It was as if I made every light all across the Western United States and all the way up the ALCAN Highway until I was about 30 miles from the Alaska border. Then it was like I could not get going.

It was raining. There was a wait for the shower. At the restaurant I forgot to get an egg for Mickey (my Poodle and travel companion). "

At this point in the conversation Art choked up for a bit. When he was able to go on he said, "I was held up. I should have been all the way across and into Alaska. Now I know why but I didn't know then. As I drove along the highway that morning I just said to the Lord, 'Lord I don't know what you have in mind for me but I'm here to serve you.'

As soon as that prayer escaped my lips I came over a rise in the road and there in front of me was an airplane sitting in the middle of the highway. I was about 27 miles from Beaver Creek in the Yukon territory.

I got out of the van and walked up to the plane. What do you think the chances are that I would know the pilot? I said, 'Well hello, Jim.'

'Art Pierpont, what brings you out this way?' the pilot said.

'I have a feeling the Lord sent me,' I said.

He worked with the Christian school where my daughter Janet and her husband Dave worked. I had met him on a previous trip. He had flown to Akron, Ohio to pick up two young ladies to help in the Christian School In Kenai. He had a broken propeller and had to make an emergency landing. They had just gotten out of the plane and they were assessing the damage and praying about what to do when I drove over the hill.

Jim said, 'I'm not sure what to do.'

I said, 'Let's have the ladies put their things in the van and I will drive them to Kenai. We will take a look at that prop.'

It would take a long time to get a new prop so we drove to Beaver Creek for a hacksaw and a measuring tape. We sawed six inches off the good prop so they would be even. A Border Patrol agent who went by Black Night helped us. I think his name was Dale.

After our repairs the pilot was able to get the plane off the ground and I took the ladies on to the 200 miles from Tok Junction to Anchorage. Later the pilot told me the plane flew better with the modified propeller.

On the way we came across a truck that had run off the road and rolled down an embankment. We were able to take the driver to Anchorage. We met an oriental man who was having trouble with his battery. He had bought a new battery, but was still having trouble. I discovered that his battery cable needed to be tightened. He was glad to be back on the road.

That evening we all stopped and enjoyed a steak dinner together compliments of the driver of the pickup truck, a woman whose name was Mrs. Leonard, I believe."

Art's remarkable tale reminded me so much of what it was like to listen to Grandpa tell one of his stories. I'm sure

Grandpa would love to have been with his little brother on the ALCAN Highway adventure. I knew it would be a story I would tell over and over again to illustrate the adventure it is to invest your life in the service of Christ.

I made a mental note to call Art again, maybe even visit him at his home in the Finger Lakes Region of New York. When I got around to calling again, I discovered that Art died only a few weeks after we talked. He was ninety years old.

Chapter 26
CARSICKNESS FORGOTTEN

Among the most difficult things to do as a pastor is to comfort those who have lost children. When a child is lost to suicide or when an infant dies or anytime even a grown son or daughter dies before their parents—it is important to comfort them. Recently a family in the church lost their boy. He was a friend of mine too. The farm was the basis of this story I made-up to comfort them:

There was a boy who always grew deathly ill of carsickness on long trips. It happened especially on the way to his grandparents home when the hills began to roll. He was in such pain, that he would complain to his father;

"Daddy, you have to do something. I think I am going to die. I can't take it anymore."

His Daddy wouldn't say much. He would just keep driving toward the farm. "Well, if you get sick, don't make a mess, son. Tell me if I need to pull over. Look outside the car. You'll be better when we get there."

Finally, mercifully, he would arrive at his grandparent's farm and his suffering would end. When he got to the farm he would take off his shoes and roll up his jeans and wade in the stream-cold water washing over his feet—

smooth rocks beneath. He would run in the grass. He would pick flowers for his mother. He would chase butterflies, fish, swim, climb trees and swing in the big tree swing hanging from the leafy maple shading the yard. He would climb the trees and he would tunnel in the hay. He would play in the corn cribs. He would wrestle the dog and tumble in the mint. He would lay on his belly in the field and eat wild strawberries. Finally, they would call him in for dinner. He wouldn't eat too much. After dinner they would put a piece of warm pie in from of him with a big glob of melting homemade ice cream.

And then as evening came he would lie on the porch and he would look up into the night sky at the bright stars. Then he would climb the wooden stairs to bed. He would crawl into the big poster-bed and lost in the soft covers with hay-scented air billowing the white curtains he would listen to the murmuring and the soft laughter of adult voices from down below and sounds of the frogs and the crickets out in the night.

Lying there with the weight of his grandmother's quilt on him he couldn't even remember what it felt like to be sick. He was so happy to be in such a wonderful place with people he loved and with people who loved him.

We may be carsick on the way but there will come a time that the beauty of eternal life and the presence of perfect love will make us forget all of it and remember it no more.

Paul said it like this: *For I consider that the sufferings of this present time are not worthy to be compared with the glory which shall be revealed in us.* (Romans 8:18)

Chapter 27
GETTING IN FOR CHRISTMAS

"How much longer, Dad?" The snowy fields are passing. We are Oohing and Ahhing over displays of lights. We slow down through small towns all dressed for the season. We are fighting our way through snow and wind and cold and ice all the way from Grand Rapids, Michigan to Licking County, Ohio. After what seems like an eternity we finally pass through the little village of Utica and then South on Route 13 to St. Louisville. Everyone is awake now. Mom combs our hair and straightens our clothes. We turn east in St. Louisville and follow the road toward the base of the hills that separate us from Christmas on the farm.

The blue lights from the instrument panel glow on my dad's intense features. We are close now but the most difficult part of the trip is just ahead. The last three miles to the farm take over an hour. The last major hill before the farm is ice covered and steep. Our car will not climb the hill. We make three or four attempts tires spinning and the Plymouth sliding back down toward the base of the hill. We are so close to warmth and home and loved ones. We are so close to the security and happiness of family all gathered for Christmas but we are stranded with a steep, icy hill between us and the farm.

Dad will have to walk for help. He pulls on his gloves, turns his hat down over his ears, buttons his coat tight against the scarf around his neck and walks to Sadie's to make a call. In few minutes he is back warming himself in the car. We wait in the cold darkness tense with anticipation.

Finally beyond the hill is a faint glow of light from a vehicle coming over the hill from the other side. We break into cheering. It is the dark silhouette of my grandpa up in the seat of his little Ford-Ferguson tractor with his coat collar turned up against the icy wind.

Grandpa backs the tractor up in front of the car and snakes a log chain to the frame of the car. He slowly pulls us up to the top of the hill. He unhooks the chain then he escorts us the last mile or so to the farm. It is a great adventure. Within a few minutes we can see the old white farmhouse nestled in the snowy valley lights glowing out from within promising warmth and love and food and laughter. Down by the spring run the spruce is wearing its coat of Christmas lights. Minutes later we are stomping off snow and bearing gifts and exchanging hugs and "Merry-Christmasing" all around.

Chapter 28
RURAL USA

Some people see Veteran's Day, Memorial Day and Independence Day as little more than bank holidays. For a couple reasons they mean more to me than that. My dad and my grandfather served in the armed forces. Grandpa served in the US Navy during WWII. He was stationed in the South Pacific on Guam. He was injured when his Jeep ran over a land mine. He carried shrapnel in his leg for the rest of his life. I'm sure I never spent a day with him that he did not make some reference to his service in the Navy. He was a patriot. Growing up during the 70's it seemed to me that Grandpa always wanted to be able to see the conflict in Southeast Asia with same simple black and white moral color he saw WWII.

Dad served in the Navy during the Korean conflict and as an Army chaplain in South Vietnam. My first Christian service assignment at Moody Bible Institute was to visit from room to room at V. A. Lakeside Hospital in Chicago.

Grandpa was in the generation that has come to be known as the Greatest Generation. These were the men who built much of what our generation and the generations to follow have taken for granted all our lives.

Memorial Day and Labor Day were the blessed bookends of summer and we tried to get to the Farm on both of those days. Labor Day was effectively the last day of summer before we got down to the business of school. Dad was a schoolteacher and we were if nothing else dutiful students so for our family there was a very pronounced difference after Labor Day and before Memorial Day.

Grandpa was a laborer and a patriot so both days had their significance, but the moral weight of Memorial Day was especially strong. Old-timers didn't call it Memorial Day. To them it was always "Decoration Day" and that was one of the things we did. In the morning on Memorial Day we sometimes went to Newark but usually went to Utica to watch the Memorial Day Parade. We were quiet and contemplative and we rose when Old Glory passed and removed our hats and put our hands over our heart.

Dad and Grandpa seemed especially sober and thoughtful and I'm sure they were making a deliberate effort to train us to appreciate our national heritage and be patriotic citizens with a sense of gratitude for the great freedoms others sacrificed to preserve for us.

I grew up through the seventies when it seemed flag etiquette was rare and patriotism was out of fashion. War protests were constantly in the news. Flags were burned in the streets. Grandpa told me that he once confronted a young man who had an American flag sewn to the seat of his pants. Grandpa said, "I've seen men die for that flag." America was boiling with anti-war sentiment and widespread ambivalence about the war in Southeast Asia. To counter that atmosphere I think Dad and Grandpa wanted to be sure that their children did not have their patriotism eroded or distorted.

In the morning on a good Memorial Day we would get to Utica in time for the parade. In the parade were perfect old cars driven by fastidious old men. There were prize-winning farm animals and blushing beauty queens. There were Sausage Queens and Gourd Queens and Corn Queens. There were queens from Bladensburg and Howard, Mt. Vernon and Fredericktown, Martinsburg and St. Louisville, in formal dresses riding in the backs of glistening convertibles. There were men young and old on vintage tractors. There were floats sponsored by churches and businesses throwing candy to children. For a few years my cousins marched in the Utica High School Marching Band or walked with the local chapter of the Future Farmers of America in their coveted short royal blue corduroy jackets.

The parade, all full of small-town Americana, would end at the cemetery. We would gather around the flagpole where the flag would be at half-staff and there would be a speech and prayers and remembrances. Then then in the afternoon they would smartly raise the flag to the top and we would visit and decorate the graves.

Dad did his best between all the distractions of brothers and sisters and cousins to teach us graveyard etiquette and point out things children might overlook, then we would all head back out to the farm.

Memorial Day was about the time of first-cutting hay. I'm sure Grandpa was glad to have additional free labor on that weekend, but never seemed like real work and Grandpa always made it seem like an almost recreational enterprise. Making hay was a wonderful event that involved the whole family. The men and boys worked through the heat of the afternoon baling and loading hay and getting it into the barn. Never in my life have I tasted sweeter water than the water from the well on the farm from the cooler in the back of the baler after an afternoon of baling in the full sun and sweat and chaff making hay.

After the hay was made it was picnic-time. Labor Day and Memorial Day would both involve picnics. We grilled thick burgers out in the yard under the maple and ate them with potato salad and baked beans and sweet, sweet, sweet corn and washed it all down with wonderfully sweet and icy-cold tea. Dessert was also ice-cold watermelon—sweet juice running down your arms.

In the evening it was usually fishing or a game of softball across the run. It was a rite of passage for a boy to be able to hit the ball up onto the road. I'm not sure I ever did that except in a thousand dreams. I'm sure my dreams were never sweeter and my childhood sleep never deeper than laying at night in the big bed in the upstairs bedroom by the open window of the old farmhouse at the close of a summer holiday.

I want each of you to be true patriots. By the time you are my age you will not be able to sit down and hear a first-hand account of WWII. I hope when you meet old veterans you will listen to their stories and buy their poppies and show them quiet honor. I hope you will stand to your feet when Old Glory passes and remove your hat and hold your hand over your heart. I hope you will lean back and sing the national anthem with all your heart.

I hope whenever you see the beautiful flag of these United States of America snapping in the breeze you will pray with all your heart for a revival of righteousness and the success of the gospel in the hearts of all Americans.

Maybe one day you can spend a quiet hour at the Wilson Cemetery and you can remember some of the men and women who helped build this great country that we so deeply love. When you sit on the porch on a quiet holiday weekend and sip a glass of tea I hope you will live in a place by God's grace where murders, muggings, rapes and robberies haven't forced the school news out of the local paper.

I hope in your heart you will know the source of our beloved country's greatness. It is a beautiful country but its greatness does not lie in its natural beauty. It is a prosperous country, but its greatness does not lie in its prosperity. It is a diverse country but its greatness does not lie in its diversity. America's greatness and prosperity stems from its conformity to the Law of God and as we stray from our allegiance to Biblical law we compromise and jeopardize that greatness.

Flag burners and people who think the phrase, "One nation under God" should be removed from the pledge of allegiance should be glad they don't have to defend their opinions on the public square with government tanks bearing down on them.

On Memorial Day when I tucked you into bed at night it would often be with a prayer that God would make true, selfless, noble, godly patriots of each of you and of your children. I wish for you the experience of hard work and sweet tea and ice cold watermelon. I hope your life is full of shade trees and soul-stirring music and stories of courage and valor. I hope you live in an America you can be proud of. I hope with your lives you contribute to that. Your grandpa and your great-grandpa would be pleased to see it.

Chapter 29
UNTO CHILDREN'S CHILDREN

It was a cold, windy, wet late October day in 1980 when they buried Grandpa. His grave is a few miles south of the little village of Chatham, Ohio, where he had entered the world seventy-two years earlier. He was buried within sight of the graves of his father and grandfather. To the west the first gentle hills of Appalachia rise from the earth. Just beyond them was the farm that was to me as much a part of him as the way he walked, though it came into his possession later in life, after his children were grown with children of their own.

I visited my grandfather's grave on a quiet afternoon the next spring. At the time I was a newlywed full of life and young. I lived with my young wife, Lois, in the western part of Ohio. I pastored a small church there in the countryside of Mercer County. While I stood there remembering him and quietly pondering time and eternity, living and dying, I noticed that the sod that had been patched in over his grave had not yet taken hold. The grass around the grave was green with life, but the sod was brown, and dry, and dead. A passage from the Psalm 103 came to my heart as I stood there that day:

As for man, his days are like grass;
As a flower of the field, so he flourishes.
For the wind passes over it, and it is gone,
And its place remembers it no more.
But the mercy of the LORD is from
everlasting to everlasting
On those who fear Him,
And His righteousness to children's children
Psalm 103:15-17 (NKJV)

Grandpa's life on earth was spent. He would no longer be the heart and life of our family gatherings. He would no longer be there to tell us of the adventures of his youth or of his exploits in life. From now on those who loved him would have to gather his stories like long-forgotten treasures from the attic, to tell them again in the best way we could.

I have kept his memory alive in my heart, his children and my cousins will not forget him as long as they are alive, but soon it will be difficult to find evidence on earth of his life. As the scripture says; "*...its place remembers it no more...*" Like blossoms that fell from the tree over thirty years ago, he is gone. When my generation is gone, others may read of Kenneth Dale Pierpont, and few will be alive who remember him, but the mercy of the Lord is forever and His righteousness can endure in his children's children. By the grace of God, righteousness will live on through generations of sons and daughters –all those who, like he did, fear God and put their faith in Christ alone.

In May, our first grandchild, a great-great grandson was born into his family. Someday I will take Kyle Kenneth to that place between Chatham and Newark, Ohio. I will show him his great, great grandfather's grave. I will take his hand and walk him across the road to see the graves of Jerome and Charles Pierpont. I will remind him that there are others who will follow him and though some day they will be forgotten, their righteousness can endure–passed on from generation to generation by the mercy of the Lord.

> *"...the mercy of the LORD is from everlasting to everlasting On those who fear Him, And His righteousness to children's children. to such as keep His covenant And to those who remember his commandments to do them."* (Psalm 103:17-18)

I cannot hope to keep the blossom of my frail life alive for long, but I can live and pray every day I am on the earth that my sons' and daughters' sons and daughters will know my grandmother's and grandfather's God.

Kenneth Dale Pierpont 1908-1980
Kenneth Frederick Pierpont 1934-
Kenneth Lee Pierpont 1958-
Kyle Dale Pierpont 1981-
Kyle Kenneth Pierpont 2007-

KEN PIERPONT

Chapter 30
GRANDPA'S BLANKET-LINED WAMMUS

In 1980 Lois and I lived in the parsonage on Swamp Road across from Beaver Chapel, the little country church I pastored at the time. It was before any of the children had come into our lives. Before the Thanksgiving Eve service we packed the car and as soon as the last parishioner drove away to finish Thanksgiving preparations we left. We would cross the state in our powder-blue VW Beetle to spend Thanksgiving Day with the family. The car never did heat well, so we had to stay bundled in blankets as we drove through the night. A light snowfall began and added adventure to our trip.

The cold and snow and lap robe gave our Thanksgiving trip an over-the-river-and-through-the-woods feel of an old-fashioned sleigh-ride. It was a happy time for a very young couple enjoying their second Thanksgiving together. For the next two and a half hours we listened to the AM radio some and talked. It was almost midnight when we arrived at the bungalow in Newark where my sister Melony, her husband Jim and family lived.

We hurried in the house through a light dusting of snow and were soon warm again. My sister had made all the arrangements for a meaningful and relaxing time. There was a fire burning when we arrived in their big, warm bungalow-style house in Newark. Scented candles were burning in our room, their fragrance blending with the aroma of pumpkin pies baking. The quilt was turned back and we were soon sleeping warmed above by a thick comforter and beneath by an electric pad.

In the morning the rest of the family drove in for the day, some from around town and others from around the state. Mom and Dad, Kevin and Nathan came from Battle Creek. The day was filled with laughter and conversation, one sentence stepping on the tail of the next.

The centerpiece of our weekend together was of course our family feast at noon on Thanksgiving Day. It was a wonderful meal with our family spilling out into two or three rooms of the house. Grandma was there. It was the first time in my life Grandma was there without Grandpa.

In October of 1980 Grandpa went out with his bow early in the deer season. It was cold and wet and he knew enough to come in but had no intention of doing so. Grandpa did not want to die in a nursing home. He contracted pneumonia and died of congestive heart failure before the trees were bare of leaves that fall. So it was Thanksgiving without Grandpa for the first time in my life.

After our feast, the men decided on a little exercise as an aid to digestion. We all went to the Roosevelt school lawn for an all-out game of tag football. It was a little cold and I needed a jacket. On the way out the door Grandma said; "here, wear this. It was your grandpa's." She handed me a Carter's denim farm chore jacket with a corduroy collar.

The working entrance of the farmhouse was a mud-room-like back porch of the kitchen in the back of the house. It was a wonderful room filled with character. There were shotguns and lanterns there. There was a shelf with shotgun shells. The was a row of wooden pegs where Grandpa would hang chore coats for every season. Some of the coats were unlined for early spring and late fall. Others had thick flannel linings that looked like old horse blankets. Grandpa always called his chore coat a "blanket-lined wammus."

It was one of these unlined coats Grandma handed me on the way out to play football. Memories flooded in when I put it on. Grandpa was a big man for his time and I was proud to be able to fill the coat. After the game I reluctantly gave the coat back to Grandma. To my delight she said; "Why don't you keep that, I think your Grandpa would want you to have it." I remembered Grandpa coming across the yard on the old farm, from the milk house with the collar of his chore-coat turned up against the wind.

I still have the coat, but it no longer fits. A couple years ago, in the fall I ran across it and gave it to Kyle, his great grandson, born a year and a week after Grandpa went to be with Lord. It pleased me to see it on him. Grandpa would have appreciated how quick Kyle is to pick up on things. He would have liked his serious nature.

Someday the coat will wear out or it will be removed from the back of his closet and sent to the second-hand store by someone who does not know its history. It may be lost and forgotten some day. But there are stories about my Grandfather's faith and the values that God was growing in him until the day of his death that should be passed down like valuable family heirlooms.

It would be wonderful to pass stately homes and valuable lands down through the generations, but that's not always possible. It would be a treasure if the farm was still in our family. It is not. But Grandpa's God is my God. His faith is my faith and when this earth as we know it is no more and a new heaven and new earth replace it, that heritage of faith can still be ours and our children's forever. I would like to leave a gold watch or a beautiful mountain lodge to my grandchildren that will come, but I would rather leave an heirloom-quality faith.

A good man leaves an inheritance to his children's children... (Proverbs 13:22 NKJV)

Chapter 31
THE GREEN DUSTER

A few years before Grandpa died, he and Grandma sold the farm. They found a nice split-level house on the edge of Newark where they lived until Grandpa died. Grandpa bought a modest bass-boat for fishing trips to Buckeye Lake. He hunted on the property of friends.

One weekend we visited and Grandpa asked Dad to come out in front of the house. We all stood there in a cluster outside the garage facing the closed door.

Dad always drove mid-sized Chrysler products. He did a lot of his own work and he was used to Plymouths and Dodges and Chryslers. When everyone was assembled in front of the garage door, Grandpa hit the garage-door opener to reveal a sporty green Plymouth Duster with broad racing stripes.

"What do you think of that?" Grandpa asked.

Dad said, "That's clean as can be. Nice little car. It's in great shape."

"That's the right answer," Grandpa said and handed him the keys.

"No. Dad I can't take this."

"We want you to have it. It's yours," Grandpa said.

Grandpa insisted on giving Dad the car. He had picked it out just for him—a small Plymouth. He knew Dad would like it. He paid cash for the car with money from the farm.

I will never forget the deep feeling of that moment. Grandpa and Grandma smiling, Dad with his head down tears running down his face. There was such love in the driveway that day.

A few years later I went to college. Dad gave me the car he had been using to commute to his school-teaching job, a powder-blue VW Beetle. The heater didn't work well. When I returned to school in January, Dad wanted me to be warm. He insisted on giving me the Duster to take back to college. Dad maintained the car, paid for the insurance and gave me a gasoline credit card and a five-dollar limit per week. Dad said, "That's enough gas to get you to work." It was a great help in my college years.

I drove back to college in the little Plymouth that Grandpa bought as a special gift to my Dad. When Lois and I married we drove away from the church and started our married life with the little Green Duster—bought with money from the farm, a sacrificial love-gift from my Grandfather to my Dad. It was a piece of the old farm. Dad gave it to me.

Chapter 32
AMONG MY BOOKS

Puttering around among my books I spot an old book of pastoral theology passed down to me from my grandpa's modest library. I take it in hand and turn it over a few times, enjoying the weight of it. Something about it tugs on my memory. I open it. Suddenly it comes back to me why this is a very special book.

Grandpa had great eyesight. He always said that when he was in the Navy he was tested and told he had rare 20/10 vision. (I guess that's twice as good as normal vision). This may have been one of the things that made Grandpa a skilled hunter. He was a keen observer of nature. I'm sure the eyesight was especially helpful.

We were on the tractor chugging up the lane aimed at the gate to the field on top of the North hill one mid-summer day when, without speaking, he stopped the tractor and pointed toward the ground.

"There's a four-leaf clover right over there. Those are pretty rare why don't you jump off and pick that."

I strained eyes. I couldn't see it. "Where, Grandpa?"

"You can't see it there? It's about two feet out to the right of the front tire."

I couldn't see it.

I noticed the wide blue sky. I saw the wispy white clouds and the colorful birds that occupied the wide blue sky. I noticed the silvery ripples in the pond in the morning breeze and the glassy surface of an evening calm. I stood in quiet meditation watching how the slanting light of the sun reflected on the water in the deepening dusk. I saw the insects that skittered on the surface of the water in the evening and the circles where the bass would rise as darkness was coming on.

I noticed the graceful way the maple leaves waved in the wind. I noticed how the leaves of the maples were minty green in early spring, a light pastel, how they would turn to a rich dark green in summer and then in the shorter days of September begin to blush with color until they displayed their full dying glory against the deep blue October sky. I noticed how by mid-November the wind would blow the maples bare to leave a stark pencil sketch where the month before there had been a beautiful watercolor of a tree.

I noticed the feathery tassels over the corn growing in artful bands on the hillsides and the green pasture growing between the bands of corn. The symmetry-the artistry of a well-groomed hill farm draws my attention to this day-how the crops lay like a mantle on the shoulders of the hills.

I noticed the country noises and the absence of suburban sounds. There was not a highway within miles. The nearest paved road was miles away—Martinsburg Road and that was a lightly-traveled undulating, curving, scenic farm road.

The farm was bisected by a gravel road. There were only a few farms on the road. The mail truck would pass once a day. Only a few cars a day passed the farm. If you were within site of the road when a car passed it would be a great social affront not to raise your head and wave your hat or hand in greeting. The locals would consider you odd and anti-social, the talk at the coffee shop would go like this; "You know I was out past the Kaylors this morning. I don't know what's gotten into him. He didn't even look up."

You could hear the tires on the gravel and unless there had been a rain within a few days a plume of dust would rise and fall after the car. Once the noise of the passing car or truck fell away the country sounds would be amplified in the quiet.

I noticed the lazy grazing of the cows and how they would always cluster together. I noticed how the cows would graze over to the fence-line in the east and eat away the low-hanging branches leaving a neatly-groomed appearance. For the rest of my life I would notice when livestock or deer would trim the trees and leave the forest with a park-like grooming along the edge of the wood.

I noticed the pasture in spring green as Ireland. I noticed the bleached white of the limestone in the lane and in the two-tracks over the hills. I noticed the blue and purple paint of the hills rolling off into the distance and the cloud of condensation left by a jet thousands of feet overhead silently streaking white across the sky.

I noticed the smell of the barn, a wonderful mix of manure, hay, grease, faint exhaust from the tractor, molasses in the feed, and ancient timber aged by moisture and sun and years. The barn on a working farm has a fragrance, a beautiful perfume you could only appreciate if you cherished a few summers in the country.

I noticed a lot of things, but Grandpa had a way of pointing out things I overlooked.

I let go of the fender and jumped down from the draw-bar where I was standing and walked over in the direction of where he was pointing and tried to search every inch of the ground. He throttled-back the engine, took the tractor out of gear, set the brakes, let out the clutch, slowly got off, walked over, bent down and picked a four-leaf clover. I watched him do this more than once. He held the clover up for me to see and then put it in the pocket of his chore coat.

At first I thought it was a prank. I thought he had a four-leaf clover in his pocket and he would do a little sleight of hand when he bent over to "pick" the four-leaf clover. I expressed my doubts so the next time he made me look at the clover and confirm it and pick it myself and hand it to him.

When we returned to the house he would walk over and pick a thick book of pastoral theology, a hardcover book with a green dust-jacket, and he would open the book and press the clover between it's pages. The book was called *Pastoral Leadership*, by Andrew Blackwood.

I've had my meetings and closed out my tasks for the day. The phone is silent. The others have gone for the day. I prepare to turn off the lights and go home for supper. The church is quiet.

In the solitude of my study I sit among my books for a few minutes holding this old book in my hands. How long has it been? I calculate the years that have passed. It's been 40 years since we found some of the clover pressed between these pages. The memory draws my heart back to the summers of my youth. I begin to slowly fan it's pages. I'm in no hurry. There are ten or twelve places I find with four-leaf clovers pressed between the pages.

For the first time ever I begin to carefully turn every page of the book to see if there was anything I have overlooked in the years my grandfather's book sat on my shelf. I find an annotation. It is my Dad's careful printing. This book had belonged to my Dad. He had given it to Grandpa and then Dad gave it to me after Grandpa's death knowing the significance it would hold.

Inside the last few pages is something I have never seen before, a number of four-leaf clovers in a cluster, maybe twelve or fourteen of them.

Grandpa would die within ten years of the afternoon we pressed the clover. A quarter of a century later we would bury Grandma next to him in the old Wilson Cemetery. I would meet and marry Lois and serve pastorates in Ohio and Michigan. Our eight children would be born and all that busy time this book would sit silently on my self unnoticed. Years would come and go.

This afternoon, enjoying the quiet luxury of my study I hold the old book in my hands and I feel a connection across the states and the decades to the little farm in the hills of Ohio and and a rare mid-summer afternoon.

I have my grandpa's old chore coat. I have his last old Scofield Reference Bible. It is a brown leather Bible with REV K D PIERPONT on the front stamped in gold foil. I have the set of *Ellicott's Commentaries* that belonged to him and I have the book on *Pastoral Leadership* by Andrew Blackwood. Between its pages are little plants of green that one day grew out of the soil that lay on the hills of the old farm. Few other physical things remain. I put the book carefully back in its place. I turn off the lights and start for home with a thoughtful heart and a thousand sacred memories.

Chapter 33
WHEN EVERYTHING IS GONE

I few years ago we returned to Ohio for a visit. On the way home we drove a few miles out of our way to visit the Wilson Cemetery. It's just off the road to Chatham. Grandpa and Grandma are buried there as are my great-grandfather William Pierpont and his wife Lilly, and my great-great grandfather Jerome Pierpont and his wife Martha. The graves are all within about fifty yards of each other. Not far away my own parents have purchased a plot and set a stone. Everything is in place but the year of their death.

Facing east from my grandfather's grave you can see the very first foothills of the Appalachian Mountains. He loved those hills so much. They are beautiful hills. Sometimes I think I have a longing for those hills bred deep within me too.

After a few quiet minutes of thankful prayer we drove north and turned off St. Route 13 and made our way back into those hills along a route I have driven a hundred times in my life and a thousand times in my mind. Holidays, lazy summer days, family days now flood back into my heart.

Rounding the last bend before the farm, at the top of the hill we looked down on the valley. The old place hasn't said Pierpont on the mailbox for over thirty years. The current owners have owned the place longer than my grandfather did.

When I started down the hill toward the farm I could immediately see that things had changed almost beyond recognition. The pastures were returning to woods, the fences we worked so hard to maintain were gone. The pond that was my grandfather's pride was gone. The hog barn and corn crib where gone. The old gas tank was gone. The cow barn and milk house were gone. I was shocked to see that even the old garage was gone. I looked for the tree down by the spring run and it still stood. I was glad. I had come a long way to get a picture of it.

The real shock came when I looked beyond and behind where the garage had stood. The huge maple where the tire swing was tied for so long was gone without a trace. The house itself was gone, completely gone. Where the raspberry patch had been, up behind the old house, stood a new house. Behind the house further up the hill was a new garage.

The farmhouse was gone as if it had never been there. Not a trace of it remained. With blinking disbelief I stopped the car, got out and stood looking on the place where the farmhouse once stood. You would never have known that for many years people had occupied a wonderful old two-story farmhouse on that spot. They had eaten and laughed and wept and loved and argued and prayed and celebrated and mourned and done the business of living in a wonderful old house that creaked in the wind. It was warm in the winter and cool under shady maples in the summer. It was fragrant with life and now the house was gone—completely gone. There was no evidence left that it had ever been there.

I fought a feeling of sadness. It's a parable of life. One by one all the things we worked for and labored to attain and maintain, all the things we lay awake at night worrying about or praying about will be gone. All the things we accumulate will be gone altogether or slowly one-by-one, but they will not last. They cannot last. And some day each of us will be gone, too.

I looked on the mailbox. The name of the new owner was there. I remembered eating watermelon in the yard after a day of baling on a summer day just like this decades ago. I remembered how the strong young men could hit the softball up over the road and over the mailbox into the garden. I remembered long summer afternoons with an old weed whip "golfing" Canada thistles from the roadside. I remembered sledding down the hill along the road and down the drive over the run into the driveway. I remembered Dolly and Skippy and Rags a homely, squat beagle mix of a dog. I remembered how they would bury groundhogs until they were "ripe" then dig them up and bring them to you and lay them at your feet like a trophy.

Teaming memories of summer grill-outs and family games, frosty windows in winter, snow-storms, autumn glory, springtime bursting with life, roiling thunderstorms coming over the hill dark with fury scrolled across the screen of my memory. Here more than anywhere ever I had learned to smell and taste and touch and see and feel the wonder of life. Here like nowhere else I felt the security of home.

One day I was reading the letter to the Hebrews when I stumbled on a poignant poetic expression in chapter thirteen. The chapter is a beautiful description of the loving discipline of a good father. The Scripture says that our fathers chastened us "for a few days" as it seemed good to them. Literally the season of our fathers training would be almost two decades, but the Scriptures call it "for a few days."

It was that way with the farm. In my youth the place seemed timeless, but our family name was only on the deed there for a couple decades... Grandma and Grandpa owned the farm from a few years before I was born until my first year of college—really just a window—just a few days. When my cousins read this book I think they will be very surprised how many stories are in my heart of the farm considering that my time there consisted of little more than weekend and holiday visits, and not more than a week or so each summer. Its place in my memory is far out of proportion to the "few days" I spent there.

I'm sure, when I stroll with my grandfather again on the forested paths of the New Earth he will be surprised how meaningful my "few days" on the farm were and how much I have written about them. He will smile to know how the stories of the farm have made their way into my messages and given color and clarity to so many spiritual truths in so many places.

At my grandfather's funeral Pastor Doyle said he was in the stands watching. As a proof-text he used the Book of Hebrews chapter eleven. He said those who are with the Lord are witnessing our "race" on earth and cheering us onward. I like to think that is what the passage means.

I wonder if he knows that I have told stories of his old hill farm in Tennessee, California, Texas, Missouri, Pennsylvania, Michigan, Ohio, Illinois and Indiana. I wonder if he knows that I have told about the Ohio farm in Mexico and Canada in Ontario on the shore of Lake Erie and on the shore of Lake Louise in the Banff Provincial Park in the Canadian Rockies?

I hope it will put a smile on his face to know that I have seen people quiet with wonder listening to stories of his humble Midwestern farm. I have seen people laugh and weep and sigh when they visit it in their imagination. The farm and its stories will always live in my heart, but our time there was only a season—it was really only a "few days."

I got in the car in silence and drank in one last long look at the farm, then I turned the key, drove down the road to the south-west border of the farm, turned and made one final, lingering pass.

I wondered if I would ever return. The farm is almost a stranger now. I have no right to it but I will never relinquish the memories I cherish there. They will always be reminders to me that the people and the memories are more to be cherished than the houses and the barns and the things we put in them. And life is short and bittersweet.

When I am tempted to live to accumulate things or when I am burdened by worry I quiet my heart and I ask myself the question that was in my mind when I drove up over the hill and left the farm behind; "When everything I have is gone, what will be left of my life?"

ACKNOWLEDGEMENTS

I acknowledge the aid of the Great Creator:

Psalms 65:9-13 *You visit the earth and water it, You greatly enrich it; The river of God is full of water; You provide their grain, For so You have prepared it. [10] You water its ridges abundantly, You settle its furrows; You make it soft with showers, You bless its growth. [11] You crown the year with Your goodness, And Your paths drip with abundance. [12] They drop on the pastures of the wilderness, And the little hills rejoice on every side. [13] The pastures are clothed with flocks; The valleys also are covered with grain; They shout for joy, they also sing.*

The farm in Licking County was a part of the fallen earth but when I wrestle in my mind with what the earth will be like one day made new with the curse removed, I imagine the farm among the gentle hills thorn-less and sinless, its beauty magnified, and its charm multiplied. If this earth is cursed, what will the blessed earth be like? As long as I remember the farm has inspired my heart Godward and I acknowledge Him for it.

I acknowledge the loving service of my brother Kevin Pierpont and his wife Carolyn. I write, but thousands have read what only a few would ever see, because Kevin has taken initiative to volunteer his skill and knowledge to make it available to them.

60229148R00096